WORKBOOK
FOR
A SYSTEMATIC
APPROACH
TO
ENGLISH WORDS
5th Edition

by

YASUSHI SHIMO
MASAHIKO TONE

SUNDAI BUNKO

はしがき

　英単語を覚えるためには，目で読み，口に出し，耳で聞き，手で書くということを繰り返すしかありません。目だけで覚えることも，耳だけで覚えることも可能でしょうが，ほとんどの人は五感をバランスよく使って覚える方が効率よく覚えられるはずです。

　本書は『システム英単語〈5訂版〉』に準拠し，書きこみ式で英語を覚えるワークブックです。『システム英単語〈5訂版〉』の <minimal phrase> を確認し，全ての単語を3回書きこめるように作られています。つまり，覚えるために「書く」という動作を繰り返すために作られた本です。当たり前のことですが，書いたことのないことを書くのはとても難しいし，書いたことがあれば書けるようになります。書くという行為を反復すれば，「書ける」ようになります。本書を手にされた方は，今日から「書く」ことを始めて，「書ける」ようになってください。

☆「システム英単語」シリーズの英単語学習システム

　人間の脳は，一度覚えたことも，そのまま放っておけばその70%を忘れてしまうと言われています。ですからどうやって効果的に再確認するかが極めて重要なのです。『システム英単語〈5訂版〉』シリーズを使って，英単語を覚え，記憶を保つためのステップを下に挙げます。もちろん，人によって時間のかけ方は違っていいですし，場合によっては順番を反対にしてもいいのですが，ひとつの典型的なモデルだと思ってください。

　なお，本書は30単語を1セクションとしていますが，もちろん2セクション，3セクションを一気に扱ってもかまいません。自分の学習時間に合わせて進めてください。また，1日でどのStepまで進めるかも自分のペースで決めてください。たとえば同じ1セクション30個の単語を，1日に1 Stepずつ5日間かけて進めてもよいですし，1日目に1st Step，2nd Stepと進めておき，2日目に3rd Step，3日目に4th Step，4日目に5th Stepへ進む，というのでもよいでしょう。要は自分のリズムに合わせればよいのです。

1st Step ＜単語と出会う＞

『システム英単語〈5訂版〉』（別売）を読んで，単語の意味，語法などを確認。

ゆっくりでよいので，納得いくまで書籍を読んでください。納得いかないことは覚えられません。

納得できたら，フレーズを声に出して読んでみてください。

↓

2nd Step ＜耳と口で覚える＞

『システム英単語〈5訂版〉CD』『同　音声ダウンロード』（別売）を聞きながら，声に出して覚える。

CDには英語フレーズが3回収録されていますから，覚えるのに最適です。

シャドウイングと言って，聞こえてくる英語とほぼ同時に口に出すと効果的です。

発音が下手でも大丈夫。とにかく大きな声で，何度も口に出すのが大事です。

↓

3rd Step ＜書いて覚える＞

『フレーズ・単語書きこみワークブック』（本書）でフレーズ・単語を3回書く。

書くときは集中して書きましょう。覚えたい，という気持ちが大事です。書き足りないと感じた場合は，納得いくまで何度でも書いてください（本書の書きこみ欄は3回分しかありませんが，「本書の使い方」にあるやり方で，何度でも使い込んでください）。たくさん書くから，書けるようになるのです。

↓

4th Step ＜単語を使う＞

『システム英単語〈5訂版対応〉チェック問題集』（別売）でチェックテスト。
一度覚えた英単語を「使う」ことは，長期記憶に有効です。チェックテストをして，自分の力で
「思い出そう」と考えることが重要なのです。能動的に使える単語（発表語彙）となれば，
長期間記憶に定着するようになります。できなかった単語は『システム英単語〈5訂版〉』で
しっかり確認しましょう。『システム英単語〈5訂版対応〉カードⅠ・Ⅱ』(別売) で
間違えた英単語のカードを抜き出して持ち歩いてください。

↓

5th Step ＜覚えていることも再確認＞

『システム英単語〈5訂版〉CD』『同　音声ダウンロード』のシャドウイングで再確認。
『システム英単語〈5訂版〉』の記事を再確認し，もう一度本書のフレーズをチェック
してください（そのために本書の各ページ上部にある日付欄は3つあるのです）。
覚えているうちに再確認，これが長期記憶を作るのです。

　これでかなりの単語が記憶に残るはずです。もちろん中には覚えづらい単語もあるでしょうが，全単語に関して これだけやれば，長文を読んでも知らない単語はほとんどなくなるでしょうし，英作文も自信を持って書ける ようになります。

　けれども，そこでやめないでください。私たちの脳は，せっかく覚えたこともやがて忘れるようにできていま す。忘れないようするためには，あまり間をおかずに繰り返し確認するしかありません。ある有名大学を調査し たところ，学生の卒業時の英語語彙は，入学時の半分ほどしかなかったそうです。これはあまりにもったいない。 せっかく苦労して覚えた英単語は，なんとしても忘れないようにして頂きたい。心配しなくても，一度覚えたこ となら，容易に再確認できるはずです。あきらめさえしなければ，英語は皆さんにとって一生便利なツールになっ てくれます。

　英語を学ぶことで，皆さんの世界が広がってゆくことを祈っています。

著者記す

『システム英単語〈5訂版対応〉フレーズ・単語書きこみワークブック』
本書の構成と使い方

★本書は『システム英単語〈5訂版〉』に準拠した，フレーズと単語の記憶を助けるための書きこみ式ワークブックです。章立てや単語番号などは単語帳に対応しています。

★第1章 Fundamental Stage ～第4章 Final Stage は，フレーズ・単語が 30 個ずつ見開きで掲載されています（章末など，一部例外もあります）。見開き1列ごとにミニマル・フレーズ→エントリー単語の順に確認してもよいですし，左右ページごとにフレーズだけ／単語だけをまとめてチェックすることもできます。

★第5章 多義語の Brush Up はフレーズのみ，巻末のジャンル別英単語は単語のみの掲載となっています。フレーズが複数ある多義語については，「2-1」「2-2」のように番号を振っています。

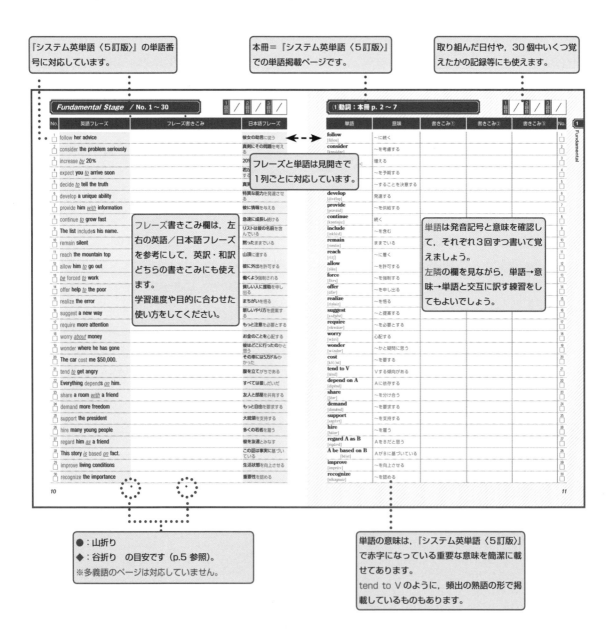

『システム英単語〈5訂版〉』の単語番号に対応しています。

本冊＝『システム英単語〈5訂版〉』での単語掲載ページです。

取り組んだ日付や，30個中いくつ覚えたかの記録等にも使えます。

フレーズと単語は見開きで1列ごとに対応しています。

フレーズ書きこみ欄は，左右の英語／日本語フレーズを参考にして，英訳・和訳どちらの書きこみにも使えます。
学習進度や目的に合わせた使い方をしてください。

単語は発音記号と意味を確認して，それぞれ3回ずつ書いて覚えましょう。
左隣の欄を見ながら，単語→意味→単語と交互に訳す練習をしてもよいでしょう。

● : 山折り
◆ : 谷折り　の目安です（p.5 参照）。
※多義語のページは対応していません。

単語の意味は，『システム英単語〈5訂版〉』で赤字になっている重要な意味を簡潔に載せてあります。
tend to V のように，頻出の熟語の形で掲載しているものもあります。

いろいろな使い方を工夫してみよう！

書きこんだ後も，折りたたんで使えばフレーズをまとめてチェックするのに便利！

単語帳付属の赤シートや下敷きなどを使って，重要ポイントをくりかえしチェック！

黒字のフレーズ・単語も別紙で隠してまるごと確認！専用のノートを作っても◎

単語帳でくわしい意味・語法の復習も忘れずに！シリーズと一緒に使えば記憶定着効果バツグン！

Contents ━━━━━━━━━━

☆（　）の中は『システム英単語〈5訂版〉』での掲載ページを表しています。

Stage 1

Fundamental Stage

"In the beginning was the Word"—— *John*

* * *

はじめに言葉ありき。—— ヨハネによる福音書

No.	英語フレーズ	フレーズ書きこみ	日本語フレーズ
1	follow her advice		彼女の助言に従う
2	consider the problem seriously		真剣にその問題を考える
3	increase *by* 20%		20%増加する
4	expect you *to* arrive soon		君がすぐ着くことを予期する
5	decide *to* tell the truth		真実を語る決意をする
6	develop a unique ability		特異な能力を発達させる
7	provide him *with* information		彼に情報を与える
8	continue *to* grow fast		急速に成長し続ける
9	The list includes his name.		リストは彼の名前を含んでいる
10	remain silent		黙ったままでいる
11	reach the mountain top		山頂に達する
12	allow him *to* go out		彼に外出を許可する
13	*be* forced *to* work		働くよう強制される
14	offer help *to* the poor		貧しい人に援助を申し出る
15	realize the error		まちがいを悟る
16	suggest a new way		新しいやり方を提案する
17	require more attention		もっと注意を必要とする
18	worry *about* money		お金のことを心配する
19	wonder where he has gone		彼はどこに行ったのかと思う
20	The car cost me $50,000.		その車には5万ドルかかった
21	tend *to* get angry		腹を立てがちである
22	Everything depends *on* him.		すべては彼しだいだ
23	share a room *with* a friend		友人と部屋を共有する
24	demand more freedom		もっと自由を要求する
25	support the president		大統領を支持する
26	hire many young people		多くの若者を雇う
27	regard him *as* a friend		彼を友達とみなす
28	This story *is* based *on* fact.		この話は事実に基づいている
29	improve living conditions		生活状態を向上させる
30	recognize the importance		重要性を認める

単語	意味	書きこみ①	書きこみ②	書きこみ③	No.
follow [fálou]	〜に続く				1
consider [kənsídər]	〜を考慮する				2
increase [inkríːs]　名 [ínkriːs]	増える				3
expect [ikspékt]	〜を予期する				4
decide [disáid]	〜することを決意する				5
develop [divéləp]	発達する				6
provide [prəváid]	〜を供給する				7
continue [kəntínjuː]	続く				8
include [inklúːd]	〜を含む				9
remain [riméin]	ままでいる				10
reach [ríːtʃ]	〜に着く				11
allow [əláu]	〜を許可する				12
force [fɔ́ːrs]	〜を強制する				13
offer [ɑ́fər]	〜を申し出る				14
realize [ríəlaiz]	〜を悟る				15
suggest [sʌdʒést]	〜と提案する				16
require [rikwáiər]	〜を必要とする				17
worry [wɔ́ːri]	心配する				18
wonder [wʌ́ndər]	〜かと疑問に思う				19
cost [kɔ́(ː)st]	〜を要する				20
tend to V [ténd]	Vする傾向がある				21
depend on A [dipénd]	Aに依存する				22
share [ʃéər]	〜を分け合う				23
demand [dimǽnd]	〜を要求する				24
support [səpɔ́ːrt]	〜を支持する				25
hire [háiər]	〜を雇う				26
regard A as B [rigɑ́ːrd]	AをBだと思う				27
A be based on B [béist]	AがBに基づいている				28
improve [imprúːv]	〜を向上させる				29
recognize [rékəgnaiz]	〜を認める				30

No.	英語フレーズ	フレーズ書きこみ	日本語フレーズ
31	notice the color change		色彩の変化に気づく
32	You _are_ supposed _to_ wear a seat belt.		シートベルトを締めることになっている
33	raise both hands		両手を上げる
34	prefer tea _to_ coffee		コーヒーよりお茶を好む
35	cheer _up_ the patients		患者たちを元気づける
36	suffer heavy damage		ひどい損害を受ける
37	describe the lost bag		なくしたバッグの特徴を言う
38	prevent him _from_ sleeping		彼が眠るのをさまたげる
39	reduce energy costs		エネルギー費を減らす
40	mistake salt _for_ sugar		塩を砂糖とまちがえる
41	prepare a room _for_ a guest		客のために部屋を準備する
42	encourage children _to_ read		子供に読書をすすめる
43	prove _to be_ true		本当だとわかる
44	treat him like a child		子供みたいに彼をあつかう
45	establish a company		会社を設立する
46	stress-related illness		ストレスと関係のある病気
47	compare Japan _with_ China		日本と中国を比較する
48	spread the tablecloth		テーブルクロスを広げる
49	What does this word refer _to_?		この語は何を指示するか
50	supply the city _with_ water		その都市に水を供給する
51	gain useful knowledge		有益な知識を得る
52	destroy forests		森林を破壊する
53	apply the rule _to_ every case		全ての場合に規則を当てはめる
54	seek help from the police		警察に助けを求める
55	search _for_ the stolen car		盗難車を捜す
56	He claims that he saw a UFO.		彼はUFOを見たと主張する
57	draw a map		地図を描く
58	refuse _to_ give up hope		希望を捨てるのを拒む
59	respond _to_ questions		質問に答える
60	Never mention it again.		二度とそのことを口にするな

(1)動詞：本冊 p. 8 〜 14

単語	意味	書きこみ①	書きこみ②	書きこみ③	No.
notice [nóutis]	〜に気づく				31
suppose [səpóuz]	〜だと思う				32
raise [réiz]	〜を上げる				33
prefer [prifə́:r]	〜をより好む				34
cheer [tʃíər]	〜を励ます				35
suffer [sʌ́fər]	〜を経験する				36
describe [diskráib]	〜を描写する				37
prevent [privént]	〜をさまたげる				38
reduce [ridjú:s]	〜を減らす				39
mistake [mistéik]	〜を誤解する				40
prepare [pripéər]	準備をする				41
encourage [inkə́:ridʒ]	はげます				42
prove [prú:v]	〜だとわかる				43
treat [trí:t]	〜をあつかう				44
establish [estǽbliʃ]	〜を設立する				45
relate [riléit]	関係がある				46
compare [kəmpéər]	〜を比較する				47
spread [spréd]	〜を広げる				48
refer to A [rifə́:r]	Aを指示する				49
supply [səplái]	〜を供給する				50
gain [géin]	〜を得る				51
destroy [distrɔ́i]	〜を破壊する				52
apply [əplái]	当てはまる				53
seek [sí:k]	〜を求める				54
search for A [sə́:rtʃ]	Aを捜す				55
claim [kléim]	〜と主張する				56
draw [drɔ́:]	〜を引っぱる				57
refuse [rifjú:z]	〜を断る				58
respond to A [rispánd]	Aに返答する				59
mention [ménʃən]	〜について述べる				60

1
Fundamental

No.	英語フレーズ	フレーズ書きこみ	日本語フレーズ
61 ☐	judge a person *by* his looks		人を外見で判断する
62 ☐	The plane is approaching Chicago.		飛行機はシカゴに接近している
63 ☐	I admit *that* I was wrong.		自分がまちがっていたと認める
64 ☐	reflect the mood of the times		時代の気分を反映する
65 ☐	perform the job		仕事を遂行する
66 ☐	a very boring movie		すごく退屈な映画
67 ☐	survive in the jungle		ジャングルで生き残る
68 ☐	Words represent ideas.		言葉は考えを表す
69 ☐	argue *that* he is right		彼は正しいと主張する
70 ☐	*take* freedom *for* granted		自由を当然と考える
71 ☐	The data indicate *that* he is right.		データは彼が正しいことを示す
72 ☐	The book belongs *to* Howard.		その本はハワードのものだ
73 ☐	acquire a language		言語を習得する
74 ☐	reply *to* his letter		彼の手紙に返事をする
75 ☐	feed a large family		大勢の家族を養う
76 ☐	escape *from* reality		現実から逃避する
77 ☐	replace the old system		古い制度に取って代わる
78 ☐	reveal a surprising fact		驚くべき事実を明らかにする
79 ☐	Japan *is* surrounded by the sea.		日本は海に囲まれている
80 ☐	The job suits you.		その仕事は君に合っている
81 ☐	the estimated population of Japan		日本の推定人口
82 ☐	aim *at* the Asian market		アジア市場をねらう
83 ☐	earn money for the family		家族のためにお金をかせぐ
84 ☐	My memory began to decline.		記憶力が低下し始めた
85 ☐	*can't* afford *to* buy a Ford		フォードの車を買う余裕がない
86 ☐	be confused by her anger		彼女の怒りに当惑する
87 ☐	graduate *from* high school		高校を卒業する
88 ☐	vary from country to country		国によって変わる
89 ☐	remove the cover		カバーを取り除く
90 ☐	insist *on* going to France		フランスに行くと言い張る

単語	意味	書きこみ①	書きこみ②	書きこみ③	No.
judge [dʒʌ́dʒ]	〜を判断する				61
approach [əpróutʃ]	（〜に）接近する				62
admit [ədmít]	〜を認める				63
reflect [riflékt]	〜を反映する				64
perform [pərfɔ́ːrm]	〜を行う				65
bore [bɔ́ːr]	〜をうんざりさせる				66
survive [sərváiv]	生き残る				67
represent [reprizént]	〜を表す				68
argue [ɑ́ːrgjuː]	〜と主張する				69
grant [grǽnt]	〜を認める				70
indicate [índikeit]	〜を指し示す				71
belong [bilɔ́(ː)ŋ]	所属している				72
acquire [əkwáiər]	〜を習得する				73
reply [riplái]	返事をする				74
feed [fíːd]	〜にエサをやる				75
escape [iskéip]	逃げる				76
replace [ripléis]	〜に取って代わる				77
reveal [rivíːl]	〜を明らかにする				78
surround [səráund]	〜を取り囲む				79
suit [súːt]	〜に合う				80
estimate [éstəmeit] 名 [éstəmət]	〜を推定する				81
aim at A [éim]	Aをねらう				82
earn [ɔ́ːrn]	〜をもうける				83
decline [dikláin]	衰退する				84
afford [əfɔ́ːrd]	〜をする余裕がある				85
confuse [kənfjúːz]	〜を当惑させる				86
graduate from A [grǽdʒueit] 名 [grǽdʒuət]	Aを卒業する				87
vary [véəri]	変わる				88
remove [rimúːv]	〜を移す				89
insist [insíst]	〜と主張する				90

No.	英語フレーズ	フレーズ書きこみ	日本語フレーズ
91	examine every record		あらゆる記録を調べる
92	remind him *of* the promise		彼に約束を思い出させる
93	contribute *to* world peace		世界平和に貢献する
94	warn him *of* the danger		彼に危険を警告する
95	connect the computer *to* the Internet		コンピュータをインターネットにつなぐ
96	match him in power		力で彼に匹敵する
97	focus *on* the problem		その問題に焦点を合わせる
98	reject the proposal		提案を拒否する
99	convince him *that* it is true		それは本当だと彼に確信させる
100	Health is associated *with* happiness.		健康は幸福と関連している
101	rush into the hospital		病院へ急いで行く
102	stress the need for information		情報の必要性を強調する
103	attract his attention		彼の注意を引きつける
104	rely *on* their power		彼らの力に頼る
105	regret leaving home		家を出たのを後悔する
106	adopt a new system		新しいシステムを採用する
107	shake the bottle well		ビンをよく振る
108	hurt her feelings		彼女の気持ちを傷つける
109	operate a computer with a mouse		マウスでコンピュータを操作する
110	Exercise extends life.		運動は寿命を延ばす
111	blame others *for* the failure		失敗を他人のせいにする
112	The book consists *of* six lessons.		その本は6課で構成されている
113	persuade them *to* go back		彼らを説得して帰らせる
114	admire her work		彼女の仕事に感嘆する
115	be disappointed *with* the test results		試験の結果に失望する
116	expand business overseas		海外へ事業を拡大する
117	preserve forests		森林を保護する
118	struggle *to* get free		自由になろうともがく
119	arrange the meeting		会議の手はずを整える
120	disturb his sleep		彼の睡眠をさまたげる

単語	意味	書きこみ①	書きこみ②	書きこみ③	No.
examine [igzǽmin]	〜を調査する				91
remind A of B [rimáind]	AにBのことを思い出させる				92
contribute to A [kəntríbjuːt]	Aに貢献する				93
warn [wɔ́ːrn]	〜に警告する				94
connect [kənékt]	〜をつなぐ				95
match [mǽtʃ]	〜に匹敵する				96
focus [fóukəs]	焦点を合わせる				97
reject [ridʒékt]	〜を断る				98
convince [kənvíns]	〜を納得させる				99
associate A with B [əsóuʃieit]	AをBに関連づける				100
rush [rʌ́ʃ]	急いで行く				101
stress [strés]	〜を強調する				102
attract [ətrǽkt]	〜を引きつける				103
rely on A [rilái]	Aに頼る				104
regret [rigrét]	〜を後悔する				105
adopt [ədápt]	〜を採用する				106
shake [ʃéik]	〜を振る				107
hurt [hɔ́ːrt]	〜を傷つける				108
operate [ápəreit]	作動する				109
extend [iksténd]	〜を広げる				110
blame [bléim]	〜を非難する				111
consist of A [kənsíst]	Aで構成されている				112
persuade [pərswéid]	〜を説得する				113
admire [ədmáiər]	〜に感心する				114
disappoint [disəpɔ́int]	〜を失望させる				115
expand [ikspǽnd]	(〜を) 拡大する				116
preserve [prizə́ːrv]	〜を保護する				117
struggle [strʌ́gl]	苦闘する				118
arrange [əréindʒ]	〜の手はずを整える				119
disturb [distə́ːrb]	〜をさまたげる				120

Fundamental Stage / No. 121 ~ 150

No.	英語フレーズ	フレーズ書きこみ	日本語フレーズ
121	employ foreign workers		外国人労働者を雇う
122	engage *in* volunteer activities		ボランティア活動に従事する
123	an abandoned pet		捨てられたペット
124	display prices		価格を示す
125	encounter many difficulties		数々の困難に出会う
126	amuse students with jokes		冗談で学生を笑わせる
127	Sorry to bother you, but ...		おじゃましてすみませんが…
128	concentrate *on* what he is saying		彼の話に集中する
129	adapt *to* a new culture		新しい文化に適応する
130	be puzzled by the problem		その問題に頭を悩ませる
131	appeal *to* his feelings		彼の感情に訴えかける
132	combine song and dance		歌と踊りを組み合わせる
133	delay his arrival		彼の到着を遅らせる
134	repair the car		車を修理する
135	a fascinating story		夢中にさせる物語
136	Pardon me.		ごめんなさい
137	import food from abroad		海外から食料を輸入する
138	remark that he is kind		彼は親切だと述べる
139	reserve a room at a hotel		ホテルの部屋を予約する
140	at an amazing speed		驚異的な速さで
141	frightening experiences		ぞっとするような経験
142	release him *from* work		仕事から彼を解放する
143	rent an apartment		アパートを借りる
144	recover *from* illness		病気から回復する
145	I suspect that he is a spy.		私は彼がスパイではないかと思う
146	deliver a message *to* a friend		友人に伝言を渡す
147	identify people by their eyes		目で人の本人確認をする
148	The office *is* located *in* the area.		オフィスはその地域にある
149	a car manufacturing company		車を製造する会社
150	occupy a high position		高い地位を占める

(1)動詞：本冊 p. 25 ～ 31

単語	意味	書きこみ①	書きこみ②	書きこみ③	No.
employ [emplɔ́i]	～を雇う				121
engage in A [engéidʒ]	Aに従事する				122
abandon [əbǽndən]	～を捨てる				123
display [displéi]	～を展示する				124
encounter [inkáuntər]	～に偶然出会う				125
amuse [əmjúːz]	～を楽しませる				126
bother [báðər]	～に面倒をかける				127
concentrate [kánsəntreit]	集中する				128
adapt [ədǽpt]	～を適応させる				129
puzzle [pʌ́zl]	～を当惑させる				130
appeal to A [əpíːl]	Aに訴える				131
combine [kəmbáin]	～を結合させる				132
delay [diléi]	～を遅らせる				133
repair [ripéər]	～を修理する				134
fascinate [fǽsəneit]	～を夢中にさせる				135
pardon [páːrdn]	～を許す				136
import [impɔ́ːrt] 名 [impɔːrt]	～を輸入する				137
remark [rimáːrk]	（～と）述べる				138
reserve [rizɔ́ːrv]	～を予約する				139
amaze [əméiz]	～を驚嘆させる				140
frighten [fráitn]	～をおびえさせる				141
release [rilíːs]	～を解放する				142
rent [rént]	～を賃借りする				143
recover from A [rikʌ́vər]	Aから回復する				144
suspect [səspékt] 名 [sʌ́spekt]	～ではないかと思う				145
deliver [dilívər]	～を配達する				146
identify [aidéntəfai]	～の正体をつきとめる				147
be located in A [lóukeitid]	Aに位置する				148
manufacture [mænjəfǽktʃər]	～を製造する				149
occupy [ákjəpai]	～を占める				150

No.	英語フレーズ	フレーズ書きこみ	日本語フレーズ
151	own a house		家を所有している
152	be exposed *to* danger		危険にさらされる
153	translate a novel *into* English		小説を英語に翻訳する
154	cure him *of* his illness		彼の病気を治す
155	perceive danger		危険に気づく
156	adjust *to* a new school		新しい学校に慣れる
157	be alarmed by the noise		その音にぎょっとする
158	assist him in his work		彼の仕事を手伝う
159	a frozen stream		凍った小川
160	spoil the party		パーティを台無しにする
161	shift gears		ギアを変える
162	be embarrassed by the mistake		そのまちがいが恥ずかしい
163	approve *of* their marriage		2人の結婚を承認する
164	weigh 65 kilograms		65キロの重さがある
165	stretch my legs		足を広げる
166	participate *in* the meeting		会議に参加する
167	exhibit Picasso's works		ピカソの作品を展示する
168	I owe my success *to* you.		私の成功はあなたのおかげだ
169	celebrate his birthday		彼の誕生日を祝う
170	trees decorated *with* lights		電球で飾られた木々
171	forgive him *for* being late		彼の遅刻を許す
172	*be* seated on the bench		ベンチで座っている
173	*be* injured in the accident		その事故で負傷する
174	sew a wedding dress		ウエディングドレスを縫う
175	the result of the test		テストの結果
176	features of human language		人類の言語の特徴
177	the problems of modern society		現代社会の問題
178	a water wheel		水車
179	put a high value on education		教育に高い価値をおく
180	the greenhouse effect of CO_2		二酸化炭素の温室効果

（1）動詞，（2）名詞：本冊 p. 31 〜 37

単語	意味	書きこみ①	書きこみ②	書きこみ③	No.
own [óun]	～を所有している				151
expose A to B [ikspóuz]	AをBにさらす				152
translate [trǽnsleit]	～を翻訳する				153
cure [kjúər]	～を治療する				154
perceive [pərsíːv]	～を知覚する				155
adjust [ədʒʌ́st]	慣れる				156
alarm [əláːrm]	～をぎょっとさせる				157
assist [əsíst]	（～を）助ける				158
freeze [fríːz]	凍りつく				159
spoil [spɔ́il]	～を台無しにする				160
shift [ʃíft]	～を変える				161
embarrass [imbǽrəs]	～を困惑させる				162
approve [əprúːv]	賛成する				163
weigh [wéi]	～の重さがある				164
stretch [strétʃ]	～を広げる				165
participate in A [pɑːrtísipeit]	Aに参加する				166
exhibit [igzíbit]	～を展示する				167
owe A to B [óu]	AはBのおかげだ				168
celebrate [séləbreit]	～を祝う				169
decorate [dékəreit]	～を装飾する				170
forgive [fərgív]	～を許す				171
be seated [síːtid]	座っている				172
injure [índʒər]	～を傷つける				173
sew [sóu]	～を縫う				174
result [rizʌ́lt]	結果				175
feature [fíːtʃər]	特徴				176
society [səsáiəti]	社会				177
wheel [hwíːl]	車輪				178
value [vǽljuː]	価値				179
effect [ifékt]	効果				180

1 Fundamental

No.	英語フレーズ	フレーズ書きこみ	日本語フレーズ
181	individuals in society		社会の中の個人
182	*have* a bad influence *on* children		子供に悪い影響を与える
183	charge a fee for the service		サービス料を請求する
184	*at* the rate of 40% a year		年40%の割合で
185	a sign of spring		春のきざし
186	water and gas service		水道とガスの事業
187	advances *in* technology		科学技術の進歩
188	Laughter is the best medicine.		笑いは最高の良薬だ
189	produce new materials		新しい物質を作る
190	a center of heavy industry		重工業の中心地
191	an attempt *to* break the record		記録を破ろうとする試み
192	US trade with France		アメリカとフランスの貿易
193	You've *made* progress *in* English.		君の英語は進歩した
194	*make* an excuse to leave early		早く帰るための言い訳をする
195	the custom of tipping		チップを払う習慣
196	Read the following passage.		次の一節を読みなさい
197	the market economy		市場経済
198	the tracks of a lion		ライオンの足跡
199	use public transportation		公共交通機関を使う
200	a government official		政府の役人
201	love at first sight		一目ぼれ
202	a taste of lemon		レモンの味
203	a wide range of information		広範囲の情報
204	make an appointment *with* the doctor		医者に予約する
205	a doctor and a patient		医者と患者
206	a business project		事業計画
207	Would you *do* me a favor?		頼みをきいてもらえませんか
208	differ in appearance		外見が違う
209	*run the* risk of losing money		お金を失う危険を冒す
210	costs and benefits of the business		仕事のコストと利益

単語	意味	書きこみ①	書きこみ②	書きこみ③	No.
individual [indəvídʒuəl]	個人				181
influence [ínfluəns]	影響				182
fee [fíː]	謝礼				183
rate [réit]	割合				184
sign [sáin]	印				185
service [sə́ːrvəs]	（公益）事業				186
advance [ədvǽns]	前進				187
laughter [lǽftər]	笑い				188
material [mətíəriəl]	物質				189
industry [índəstri]	工業				190
attempt [ətémpt]	試み				191
trade [tréid]	貿易				192
progress [prágres] 動 [prəgrés]	進歩				193
excuse [ikskjúːs] 動 [ikskjúːz]	言い訳				194
custom [kʌ́stəm]	習慣				195
passage [pǽsidʒ]	一節				196
economy [ikánəmi]	経済				197
track [trǽk]	小道				198
transportation [trænspərtéiʃən]	交通機関				199
official [əfíʃəl]	役人				200
sight [sáit]	見ること				201
taste [téist]	味				202
range [réindʒ]	範囲				203
appointment [əpɔ́intmənt]	約束				204
patient [péiʃənt]	患者				205
project [prádʒekt] 動 [prədʒékt]	計画				206
favor [féivər]	好意				207
appearance [əpíərəns]	外見				208
risk [rísk]	危険				209
benefit [bénəfit]	利益				210

No.	英語フレーズ	フレーズ書きこみ	日本語フレーズ
211	residents of New York		ニューヨークの住民
212	their relatives and friends		彼らの親戚と友達
213	a mountain region		山岳地方
214	unique characteristics		ユニークな特徴
215	feel a sharp pain		鋭い痛みを感じる
216	a pair of *identical* twins		一組の一卵性双生児
217	*on* special occasions		特別な場合に
218	the principle of free trade		自由貿易の原則
219	the history department		歴史学科
220	It is my duty to help you.		君を助けるのが私の義務だ
221	the scene of the accident		事故の現場
222	avoid *traffic* jams		交通渋滞を避ける
223	the spirit of fair play		フェアプレーの精神
224	the medium of communication		コミュニケーションの手段
225	mass production		大量生産
226	gather a large audience		大勢の観客を集める
227	the most important element		最も重要な要素
228	global climate change		地球規模の気候変動
229	the French Revolution		フランス革命
230	the first quarter of this century		今世紀の最初の4分の1
231	a room with little furniture		家具の少ない部屋
232	the human brain		人間の脳
233	CO_2 in the earth's atmosphere		地球の大気中の二酸化炭素
234	private property		私有財産
235	a reward *for* hard work		努力の報酬
236	national security		国家の安全保障
237	give a cry of delight		喜びの声をあげる
238	a deserted road in the desert		砂漠の人影のない道
239	people from different backgrounds		経歴の違う人々
240	a trend *toward* fewer children		少子化の傾向

単語	意味	書きこみ①	書きこみ②	書きこみ③	No.
resident [rézidənt]	住民				211
relative [rélətiv]	親族				212
region [ríːdʒən]	地域				213
characteristic [kærəktərístik]	特徴				214
pain [péin]	苦痛				215
twin [twín]	双子の一方				216
occasion [əkéiʒən]	場合				217
principle [prínsəpl]	原理				218
department [dipáːrtmənt]	部門				219
duty [djúːti]	義務				220
scene [síːn]	場面				221
jam [dʒǽm]	渋滞				222
spirit [spírət]	精神				223
medium [míːdiəm]	手段				224
mass [mǽs]	一般大衆				225
audience [ɔ́ːdiəns]	聴衆				226
element [éləmənt]	要素				227
climate [kláimit]	気候				228
revolution [revəljúːʃən]	革命				229
quarter [kwɔ́ːrtər]	4分の1				230
furniture [fɔ́ːrnitʃər]	家具				231
brain [bréin]	脳				232
atmosphere [ǽtməsfiər]	大気				233
property [prápərti]	財産				234
reward [riwɔ́ːrd]	報酬				235
security [sikjúərəti]	安全				236
delight [diláit]	大喜び				237
desert [dézərt] 動 [dizɔ́ːrt]	砂漠				238
background [bǽkgraund]	背景				239
trend [trénd]	傾向				240

No.	英語フレーズ	フレーズ書きこみ	日本語フレーズ
241	get 20% of the vote		20%の票を得る
242	a negative impact *on* the environment		環境に対する悪い影響
243	educational institutions		教育機関
244	social interaction *with* others		他人との社会的交流
245	an alternative *to* oil		石油の代わりになるもの
246	*do* no harm *to* children		子供に害を与えない
247	a travel agency		旅行代理店
248	people's great capacity *to* learn		人間のすばらしい学習能力
249	the Italian minister		イタリアの大臣
250	a hospital volunteer		病院で働くボランティア
251	*have* access *to* the Internet		インターネットを利用できる
252	large quantities *of* data		ぼう大な量のデータ
253	a branch *of* science		科学の一分野
254	a common language		共通の言語
255	a rough sketch		大ざっぱなスケッチ
256	He *is* likely *to* win.		彼が勝つ可能性が高い
257	scrious social problems		深刻な社会問題
258	a particular character		特有の性質
259	information available *to* everyone		みんなが利用できる情報
260	bilingual children		二言語使用の子どもたち
261	I *am* ready *to* start.		出発の用意ができている
262	the correct answer		正しい答え
263	be familiar *with* Japanese culture		日本の文化にくわしい
264	physical beauty		肉体美
265	The book is worth read*ing*.		その本は読む価値がある
266	be involved *in* the accident		事故に巻き込まれている
267	I had a fantastic time.		私はすばらしい時をすごした
268	her private life		彼女の私生活
269	an obvious mistake		明白なまちがい
270	a native language		母語

単語	意味	書きこみ①	書きこみ②	書きこみ③	No.
vote [vóut]	投票				241
impact [ímpækt]	影響				242
institution [ìnstətjúːʃən]	機関				243
interaction [ìntərǽkʃən]	交流				244
alternative [ɔːltə́ːrnətiv]	代わりのもの				245
harm [háːrm]	害				246
agency [éidʒənsi]	機関				247
capacity [kəpǽsəti]	能力				248
minister [mínəstər]	大臣				249
volunteer [vὰləntíər]	ボランティア				250
access [ǽkses] [æksés]	利用する権利				251
quantity [kwántəti]	量				252
branch [brǽntʃ]	枝				253
common [kámən]	共通の				254
rough [rʌ́f]	荒い				255
likely [láikli]	ありそうな				256
serious [síəriəs]	深刻な				257
particular [pərtíkjulər]	ある特定の				258
available [əvéiləbl]	手に入る				259
bilingual [bailíŋgwl]	二言語使用の				260
ready [rédi]	用意ができた				261
correct [kərékt]	正しい				262
familiar [fəmíljər]	よく知られた				263
physical [fízikəl]	身体の				264
be worth A [wə́ːrθ]	Aの価値がある				265
be involved in A [inválvd]	Aに関係している				266
fantastic [fæntǽstik]	すばらしい				267
private [práivit]	個人の				268
obvious [ábviəs]	明白な				269
native [néitiv]	母国の				270

No.	英語フレーズ	フレーズ書きこみ	日本語フレーズ
271	a complex system		複雑なシステム
272	I'm willing *to* pay for good food.		おいしいものにお金を払ってもかまわない
273	the current international situation		今日の国際状況
274	male workers		男性の労働者
275	the proper use of words		言葉の適切な使い方
276	He is capable *of* doing the job.		彼はその仕事をする能力がある
277	He is independent *of* his parents.		彼は親から独立している
278	positive thinking		積極的な考え方
279	a pleasant experience		楽しい経験
280	a significant difference		重要な違い
281	the former president		前大統領
282	a chemical reaction		化学反応
283	be upset by the accident		事故で動揺している
284	from the previous year		前の年から
285	keep calm		冷静でいる
286	a specific individual		特定の個人
287	health-conscious Americans		健康を意識するアメリカ人
288	be superior *to* others		他の人よりすぐれている
289	an efficient use of energy		効率のよいエネルギーの使い方
290	fundamental human rights		基本的人権
291	a narrow street		狭い通り
292	a reasonable explanation		理にかなった説明
293	feel nervous about the future		将来のことで不安になる
294	The brothers look alike.		その兄弟は似ている
295	domestic violence		家庭内暴力
296	a negative answer		否定的な答え
297	make a moral judgment		道徳的な判断をする
298	be eager *to* study in the US		アメリカ留学を熱望する
299	the brain's remarkable ability		脳のすばらしい能力
300	drive away evil spirits		悪い霊を追い払う

単語	意味	書きこみ①	書きこみ②	書きこみ③	No.
complex [kɑmpléks] 名 [kámpleks]	複雑な				271
be willing to V [wíliŋ]	Vする気がある				272
current [kə́:rənt]	最新の				273
male [méil]	男の				274
proper [prɑ́pər]	適切な				275
capable [kéipəbl]	〜する能力がある				276
independent [indipéndənt]	独立した				277
positive [pázitiv]	積極的な				278
pleasant [plézənt]	楽しい				279
significant [signífikənt]	重要な				280
former [fɔ́:rmər]	前の				281
chemical [kémikəl]	化学的な				282
upset [ʌpsét]	動揺している				283
previous [prí:viəs]	前の				284
calm [kά:m]	冷静な				285
specific [spəsífik]	特定の				286
conscious [kάnʃəs]	意識している				287
superior [supíəriər]	よりすぐれている				288
efficient [ifíʃənt]	効率がいい				289
fundamental [fʌndəméntəl]	基本的な				290
narrow [nǽrou]	狭い				291
reasonable [rí:znəbl]	理にかなった				292
nervous [nə́:rvəs]	神経質な				293
alike [əláik]	似ている				294
domestic [dəméstik]	家庭の				295
negative [négətiv]	否定の				296
moral [mɔ́(:)rəl]	道徳的な				297
eager [í:gər]	熱心な				298
remarkable [rimά:rkəbl]	すばらしい				299
evil [í:vəl]	悪い				300

No.	英語フレーズ	フレーズ書きこみ	日本語フレーズ
301	stay awake all night		夜通し目が覚めている
302	his aged parents		彼の年老いた父母
303	I am anxious *about* your health.		君の健康が心配だ
304	a tough boxer		たくましいボクサー
305	nuclear energy		原子力エネルギー
306	the British legal system		イギリスの法律の制度
307	be curious *about* everything		何にでも好奇心を持つ
308	civil rights		市民権
309	according to a recent study		最近の研究によると
310	a senior member of the club		クラブの先輩の部員
311	Soon afterward, he left.		その後すぐ彼は去った
312	nearly 30 years ago		30年近く前に
313	The car is small and therefore cheap.		その車は小さい。それゆえ安い。
314	at exactly *the same* time		ぴったり同時に
315	He will possibly come.		ひょっとすると彼は来るかもしれない
316	contrary *to* expectations		予想に反して
317	I occasionally go to the theater.		私はたまに劇場に行く
318	Somehow I feel lonely.		なぜか寂しい
319	I seldom see him.		彼に会うことはめったにない
320	This is smaller and thus cheaper.		この方が小さく, したがって安い
321	people throughout the world		世界中の人々
322	Unlike my wife, I get up early.		妻と違って私は早起きだ
323	Besides being rich, he is kind.		彼は金持ちの上にやさしい
324	It's beyond my understanding.		私の理解をこえている
325	within a mile *of* the station		駅から1マイル以内で
326	have *neither* time nor money		時間もお金もない
327	I'll leave tomorrow unless it rains.		明日雨が降らない限り出発する
328	work *every* day except Sunday		日曜以外毎日働く
329	You ought *to* see a doctor.		君は医者に診てもらうべきだ
330	*in* spite *of* difficulties		困難にもかかわらず

⑶形容詞，⑷副詞・その他：本冊 p. 60 〜 67

単語	意味	書きこみ①	書きこみ②	書きこみ③	No.
awake [əwéik]	目を覚まして				301
aged [éidʒid]	年老いた				302
anxious [ǽŋkʃəs]	心配して				303
tough [tʌ́f]	たくましい				304
nuclear [njúːkliər]	核の				305
legal [líːgəl]	合法の				306
curious [kjúəriəs]	好奇心が強い				307
civil [sívl]	一般市民の				308
recent [ríːsnt]	最近の				309
senior [síːnjər]	上級の				310
afterward [ǽftərwərd]	その後				311
nearly [níərli]	ほとんど				312
therefore [ðéərfɔːr]	それゆえに				313
exactly [igzǽktli]	正確に				314
possibly [pάsəbli]	ひょっとすると				315
contrary [kάntrəri]	反対に				316
occasionally [əkéiʒənəli]	時々				317
somehow [sʌ́mhau]	どういうわけか				318
seldom [séldəm]	めったに〜ない				319
thus [ðʌ́s]	それゆえ				320
throughout [θru(ː)áut]	前 〜のいたる所に				321
unlike [ʌnláik]	前 〜と違って				322
besides [bisáidz]	前 〜に加えて				323
beyond [bijάnd]	前 〜の向こうに				324
within [wiðín]	前 以内で				325
nor [nɔ́ːr]	接 〜もない				326
unless [ənlés]	接 〜しない限り				327
except [iksépt]	前 接 〜を除いて				328
ought to V [ɔ́ːt]	助 Vすべきである				329
in spite of [spáit]	前 〜にもかかわらず				330

1 Fundamental

No.	英語フレーズ	フレーズ書きこみ	日本語フレーズ
331	I don't know *whether* it is true *or not*.		本当かどうかわからない
332	explain *why* he was late		彼がなぜ遅れたかを説明する
333	accept the truth as it is		ありのまま真実を受け入れる
334	produce enough food		十分な食料を生産する
335	Does God really exist?		神は本当に存在するのか
336	express my feelings		私の気持ちを表現する
337	add some milk *to* the soup		スープにミルクを加える
338	avoid mak*ing* mistakes		まちがいを犯すのを避ける
339	marry Mary		メアリと結婚する
340	protect children *from* danger		危険から子供たちを守る
341	Alcohol affects the brain.		アルコールは脳に影響する
342	determine your future		君の未来を決定する
343	solve the problem		問題を解決する
344	Vegetables contain a lot of water.		野菜はたくさんの水を含んでいる
345	discuss the problem with him		彼とその問題を議論する
346	ignore the doctor's advice		医者の忠告を無視する
347	guess how old she is		彼女の年を推測する
348	exchange yen *for* dollars		円をドルに交換する
349	satisfy the needs of students		学生の要求を満たす
350	complain *about* the noise		騒音のことで苦情を言う
351	finally achieve the goal		ついに目標を達成する
352	enable people *to* live longer		人々の長寿を可能にする
353	intend *to* live in America		アメリカに住むつもりだ
354	obtain information about him		彼に関する情報を得る
355	divide the cake *into* six pieces		ケーキを6個に分割する
356	The noise annoys me.		その音が私をいらだたせる
357	My opinion differs *from* hers.		私の考えは彼女と異なる
358	how to educate children		子供を教育する方法
359	borrow a book *from* a friend		友達から本を借りる
360	invent a time machine		タイムマシンを発明する

単語	意味	書きこみ①	書きこみ②	書きこみ③	No.
whether [hwéðər]	接 ～かどうか				331
explain [ikspléin]	～を説明する				332
accept [əksépt]	～を受け入れる				333
produce [prədjúːs]	～を生産する				334
exist [igzíst]	存在する				335
express [iksprés]	～を表現する				336
add [ǽd]	～を加える				337
avoid [əvɔ́id]	～を避ける				338
marry [mǽri]	～と結婚する				339
protect [prətékt]	～を守る				340
affect [əfékt]	～に影響する				341
determine [ditə́ːrmin]	～を決定する				342
solve [sálv]	～を解決する				343
contain [kəntéin]	～を含んでいる				344
discuss [diskʌ́s]	～を議論する				345
ignore [ignɔ́ːr]	～を無視する				346
guess [gés]	～を推測する				347
exchange [ikstʃéindʒ]	交換する				348
satisfy [sǽtisfai]	～を満たす				349
complain [kəmpléin]	苦情を言う				350
achieve [ətʃíːv]	～を達成する				351
enable [inéibl]	～を可能にする				352
intend [inténd]	～を意図する				353
obtain [əbtéin]	～を得る				354
divide [diváid]	分割する				355
annoy [ənɔ́i]	～をいらだたせる				356
differ [dífər]	異なる				357
educate [édʒukeit]	～を教育する				358
borrow [bárou]	～を借りる				359
invent [invént]	～を発明する				360

No.	英語フレーズ	フレーズ書きこみ	日本語フレーズ
361	promote economic growth		経済成長を促進する
362	advise him *to* eat vegetables		野菜を食べるよう彼に忠告する
363	retire *from* work at sixty		60で仕事を辞める
364	permit him *to* go out		彼に外出することを許す
365	recommend this book *to* you		あなたにこの本を勧める
366	apologize *to* him *for* being late		遅れたことを彼に謝る
367	inform him *of* his son's success		息子の成功を彼に知らせる
368	oppose their marriage		彼らの結婚に反対する
369	trust an old friend		古い友達を信用する
370	select the best answer		最良の答えを選ぶ
371	praise him *for* his work		仕事のことで彼をほめる
372	how to handle problems		どう問題に対処するべきか
373	propose a new way		新しいやり方を提案する
374	breathe fresh air		新鮮な空気を呼吸する
375	criticize him *for* being late		遅刻したことで彼を非難する
376	overcome difficulties		困難に打ち勝つ
377	possess great power		大きな力を持っている
378	predict the future		未来を予言する
379	publish a book		本を出版する
380	leaves floating on the river		川面に浮かぶ木の葉
381	recall the good old days		古き良き時代を思い出す
382	explore the Amazon River		アマゾン川を探検する
383	pretend *to* be asleep		眠っているふりをする
384	absorb a lot of water		大量の水を吸収する
385	He resembles his father.		彼は父親に似ている
386	tear the letter to pieces		ずたずたに手紙を引き裂く
387	consume a lot of energy		多量のエネルギーを消費する
388	compete *with* him *for* the gold medal		金メダルを目指して彼と競争する
389	quit smok*ing*		タバコをやめる
390	announce a new plan		新しい計画を発表する

(5)動詞：本冊 p. 74 〜 78

単語	意味	書きこみ①	書きこみ②	書きこみ③	No.
promote [prəmóut]	～を促進する				361
advise [ədváiz]	～に忠告する				362
retire [ritáiər]	辞める				363
permit [pərmít]	～を許す				364
recommend [rekəménd]	～を勧める				365
apologize [əpúlədʒaiz]	謝る				366
inform [infɔ́ːrm]	～に知らせる				367
oppose [əpóuz]	～に反対する				368
trust [trʌ́st]	～を信用する				369
select [səlékt]	～を選ぶ				370
praise [préiz]	～をほめる				371
handle [hǽndl]	～に対処する				372
propose [prəpóuz]	～を提案する				373
breathe [bríːð]	～を呼吸する				374
criticize [krítəsaiz]	～を非難する				375
overcome [ouvərkʌ́m]	～に打ち勝つ				376
possess [pəzés]	～を持っている				377
predict [pridíkt]	～を予言する				378
publish [pʌ́bliʃ]	～を出版する				379
float [flóut]	浮かぶ				380
recall [rikɔ́ːl]	～を思い出す				381
explore [iksplɔ́ːr]	～を探検する				382
pretend [priténd]	ふりをする				383
absorb [əbzɔ́ːrb]	～を吸収する				384
resemble [rizémbl]	～に似ている				385
tear [téər]	～を引き裂く				386
consume [kənsjúːm]	～を消費する				387
compete [kəmpíːt]	競争する				388
quit [kwít]	～をやめる				389
announce [ənáuns]	～を発表する				390

No.	英語フレーズ	フレーズ書きこみ	日本語フレーズ
391	react quickly *to* light		光にすばやく反応する
392	wander around the streets		街を歩き回る
393	Don't text while driving.		運転中にメールを送るな
394	generate electricity		電力を生み出す
395	score 10 goals		10点を取る
396	the Japanese government		日本政府
397	have little knowledge of English		英語の知識がほとんどない
398	the Asian nations		アジアの諸国
399	*make* an effort *to* help him		彼を助けようと努力する
400	the Cold War period		冷戦時代
401	population growth		人口の増加
402	*for* peaceful purposes		平和的な目的で
403	study human behavior		人間の行動を研究する
404	lack of food		食糧不足
405	learn basic skills		基本的な技術を学ぶ
406	the sound quality of the CD		CDの音質
407	*the* natural environment		自然環境
408	*play* an important role		重要な役割を果たす
409	a positive attitude *toward* life		人生に対する前向きな態度
410	the author of this passage		この文章の筆者
411	scientific research		科学的な研究
412	an opportunity *to* talk to her		彼女と話す機会
413	a source of information		情報源
414	carbon dioxide		二酸化炭素
415	the shape of her nose		彼女の鼻の形
416	the advantage *of* membership		会員の利点
417	a method of teaching English		英語を教える方法
418	be in the habit of reading in bed		ベッドで本を読む習慣がある
419	remember the details of the story		話を細部まで覚えている
420	within walking distance of my house		私の家から歩ける距離で

単語	意味	書きこみ①	書きこみ②	書きこみ③	No.
react [ri(:)ǽkt]	反応する				391
wander [wándər]	歩き回る				392
text [tékst]	メールを送る				393
generate [dʒénəreit]	～を生み出す				394
score [skɔ́ːr]	～を取る				395
government [gʌ́vərnmənt]	政府				396
knowledge [nálidʒ]	知識				397
nation [néiʃən]	国				398
effort [éfərt]	努力				399
period [píəriəd]	時代				400
population [pɑpjuléiʃən]	人口				401
purpose [pɔ́ːrpəs]	目的				402
behavior [bihéivjər]	行動				403
lack [lǽk]	不足				404
skill [skíl]	技術				405
quality [kwálɒti]	質				406
environment [inváiərənmənt]	環境				407
role [róul]	役割				408
attitude [ǽtitjuːd]	態度				409
author [ɔ́ːθər]	筆者				410
research [rísəːrtʃ]	研究				411
opportunity [ɑpərtjúnəti]	機会				412
source [sɔ́ːrs]	源				413
carbon [káːrbən]	炭素				414
shape [ʃéip]	形				415
advantage [ədvǽntidʒ]	利点				416
method [méθəd]	方法				417
habit [hǽbit]	習慣				418
detail [díːteil]	細部				419
distance [dístəns]	距離				420

No.	英語フレーズ	フレーズ書きこみ	日本語フレーズ
421	A large crowd gathered.		大群衆が集まった
422	the best known instance		最もよく知られた例
423	a strong desire _to_ be a singer		歌手になりたいという強い願望
424	the standard of living		生活水準
425	a difficult task		難しい仕事
426	for future generations		未来の世代のために
427	_take_ responsibility _for_ the accident		事故の責任をとる
428	experiments with animals		動物を用いる実験
429	a professional athlete		プロの運動選手
430	only a decade ago		ほんの10年前に
431	a loss of $5,000		5,000ドルの損失
432	have a high fever		高熱を出している
433	the theory of relativity		相対性理論
434	read the following statement		次の記述を読む
435	a professor at Boston University		ボストン大学の教授
436	the basic functions of a computer		コンピュータの基本的機能
437	the surface of the earth		地球の表面
438	put the letter in a pink envelope		ピンクの封筒に手紙を入れる
439	an international organization		国際的な組織
440	Japan's foreign policy		日本の外交政策
441	natural resources		天然資源
442	the contrast between light and shadow		光と影の対比
443	a flood of information		情報の洪水
444	look for a mate		連れ合いを探す
445	buying and selling goods		商品の売り買い
446	humans and other creatures		人間と他の動物
447	changes in social structure		社会構造の変化
448	history and tradition		歴史と伝統
449	lose weight		体重を減らす
450	give money to charity		慈善のために寄付する

1 Fundamental

単語	意味	書きこみ①	書きこみ②	書きこみ③	No.
crowd [kráud]	群衆				421
instance [ínstəns]	例				422
desire [dizáiər]	願望				423
standard [stǽndərd]	水準				424
task [tǽsk]	仕事				425
generation [dʒenəréiʃən]	世代				426
responsibility [rispɑnsəbíləti]	責任				427
experiment [ikspérimənt]	実験				428
athlete [ǽθliːt]	運動選手				429
decade [dékeid]	10年				430
loss [lɔ́(ː)s]	損失				431
fever [fíːvər]	熱				432
theory [θíəri]	理論				433
statement [stéitmənt]	記述				434
professor [prəfésər]	教授				435
function [fʌ́ŋkʃən]	機能				436
surface [sə́ːrfis]	表面				437
envelope [énvəloup]	封筒				438
organization [ɔːrgənizéiʃən]	組織				439
policy [pɑ́lisi]	政策				440
resource [ríːsɔːrs]	資源				441
contrast [kɑ́ntræst] 動 [kəntrǽst]	対比				442
flood [flʌ́d]	洪水				443
mate [méit]	連れ合い				444
goods [ɡúdz]	商品				445
creature [kríːtʃər]	動物				446
structure [strʌ́ktʃər]	構造				447
tradition [trədíʃən]	伝統				448
weight [wéit]	体重				449
charity [tʃǽrəti]	慈善				450

No.	英語フレーズ	フレーズ書きこみ	日本語フレーズ
451	the average American citizen		平均的アメリカ市民
452	*make* a good impression *on* him		彼によい印象を与える
453	a popular cartoon character		人気マンガのキャラクター
454	a long career as an actress		女優としての長い経歴
455	a site for a new hotel		新しいホテルの用地
456	train passengers		列車の乗客
457	violence on TV		テレビにおける暴力
458	low-income families		低所得の家族
459	the average temperature in Paris		パリの平均気温
460	*the* majority *of* students		大多数の学生
461	the origin of language		言語の起源
462	study English literature		英文学を研究する
463	office equipment		オフィスの設備
464	talk to a stranger		見知らぬ人に話しかける
465	strength and weakness		強さと弱さ
466	the planet Earth		地球という惑星
467	Truth is stranger than fiction.		事実は小説よりも奇なり
468	science and religion		科学と宗教
469	environmental pollution		環境汚染
470	wealth and power		富と権力
471	sign an official document		公文書にサインする
472	make a $2 million profit		200万ドルのもうけを得る
473	the technique of film-making		映画作りの技術
474	express emotions		感情を表現する
475	a natural phenomenon		自然現象
476	a horror movie		恐怖映画
477	climb a ladder		はしごを登る
478	8 billion people		八十億の人々
479	the social status of women		女性の社会的地位
480	modern youth		現代の若者

(6) 名詞：本冊 p. 87 〜 90

1 Fundamental

単語	意味	書きこみ①	書きこみ②	書きこみ③	No.
citizen [sítizn]	市民				451
impression [impréʃən]	印象				452
cartoon [kɑːrtúːn]	マンガ				453
career [kəríər]	経歴				454
site [sáit]	用地				455
passenger [pǽsendʒər]	乗客				456
violence [váiələns]	暴力				457
income [ínkʌm]	所得				458
temperature [témpərətʃər]	気温				459
majority [mədʒɔ́(ː)rəti]	大多数				460
origin [ɔ́(ː)ridʒin]	起源				461
literature [lítərətʃər]	文学				462
equipment [ikwípmənt]	設備				463
stranger [stréindʒər]	見知らぬ人				464
strength [stréŋkθ]	強さ				465
planet [plǽnit]	惑星				466
fiction [fíkʃən]	小説				467
religion [rilídʒən]	宗教				468
pollution [pəljúːʃən]	汚染				469
wealth [wélθ]	富				470
document [dákjumənt]	文書				471
profit [práfit]	もうけ				472
technique [tekníːk]	技術				473
emotion [imóuʃən]	感情				474
phenomenon [finámənɑn]	現象				475
horror [hɔ́(ː)rər]	恐怖				476
ladder [lǽdər]	はしご				477
billion [bíljən]	十億				478
status [stéitəs]	地位				479
youth [júːθ]	若者				480

41

No.	英語フレーズ	フレーズ書きこみ	日本語フレーズ
481	have confidence *in* my ability		自分の能力に自信がある
482	the edge of the Pacific Ocean		太平洋の周辺
483	household goods		家庭用品
484	a great scholar		偉大な学者
485	according to a new survey		新しい調査によると
486	a vocabulary of 5,000 words		5,000語の語彙
487	a natural enemy		天敵
488	a bridge *under* construction		建設中の橋
489	a lecture *on* history		歴史に関する講義
490	follow his instructions		彼の指示に従う
491	get over the economic crisis		経済危機を乗り越える
492	a dentist's instrument		歯医者の道具
493	grow various crops		さまざまな作物を育てる
494	a laser weapon		レーザー兵器
495	an electronic device		電子装置
496	the path *to* victory		勝利への道
497	predict earthquakes		地震を予知する
498	a clear mountain stream		きれいな山の小川
499	the notion of freedom		自由の概念
500	a tree in the yard		庭の木
501	victims of the war		戦争の犠牲者
502	run out of fuel		燃料を使い果たす
503	the common ancestors of all humans		すべての人類の共通の祖先
504	the rich soil of the Nile River		ナイル川の豊かな土壌
505	a debate on education		教育についての討論
506	a violent crime		凶悪犯罪
507	my friends and colleagues		私の友人と同僚
508	take a book from the shelf		たなから本を取る
509	analysis *of* DNA		DNAの分析
510	stars in the universe		宇宙の星

単語	意味	書きこみ①	書きこみ②	書きこみ③	No.
confidence [kánfidəns]	自信				481
edge [édʒ]	周辺				482
household [háushould]	家庭				483
scholar [skálər]	学者				484
survey [sə́ːrvei] 動 [sərvéi]	調査				485
vocabulary [voukǽbjəleri]	語彙				486
enemy [énəmi]	敵				487
construction [kənstrʌ́kʃən]	建設				488
lecture [léktʃər]	講義				489
instruction [instrʌ́kʃən]	指示				490
crisis [kráisis]	危機				491
instrument [ínstrəmənt]	道具				492
crop [krɑ́p]	作物				493
weapon [wépən]	兵器				494
device [diváis]	装置				495
path [pǽθ]	道				496
earthquake [ə́ːrθkweik]	地震				497
stream [stríːm]	小川				498
notion [nóuʃən]	概念				499
yard [jɑ́ːrd]	庭				500
victim [víktim]	犠牲者				501
fuel [fjúː(ː)əl]	燃料				502
ancestor [ǽnsestər]	祖先				503
soil [sɔ́il]	土壌				504
debate [dibéit]	討論				505
crime [kráim]	犯罪				506
colleague [káliːg]	同僚				507
shelf [ʃélf]	たな				508
analysis [ənǽlisis]	分析				509
universe [júːnəvəːrs]	宇宙				510

No.	英語フレーズ	フレーズ書きこみ	日本語フレーズ
511	a machine run by electricity		電気で動く機械
512	social insects like ants		アリのような社会性昆虫
513	be caught in a spider's web		クモの巣にかかる
514	a heavy storm		激しい嵐
515	have plenty _of_ time		十分な時間がある
516	land suitable for agriculture		農業に向いた土地
517	the gene for eye color		目の色を決める遺伝子
518	evidence of life on Mars		火星に生物がいるという証拠
519	_have_ serious consequences		重大な結果をまねく
520	the mother-infant relationship		母親と幼児の関係
521	have no leisure time for sports		スポーツをする暇がない
522	the gray cells of the brain		灰色の脳細胞
523	have musical talent		音楽の才能がある
524	newspaper advertising		新聞広告
525	increase _to_ some extent		ある程度まで増える
526	take out the garbage		ゴミを出す
527	the general public		一般人衆
528	various kinds of flowers		さまざまな種類の花
529	be similar _to_ each other		お互いに似ている
530	a complete failure		完全な失敗
531	a sharp rise in prices		物価の急激な上昇
532	an expensive restaurant		高価なレストラン
533	a political leader		政治的な指導者
534	be aware _of_ the danger		危険に気づいている
535	ancient Greece and Rome		古代のギリシャとローマ
536	a medical study		医学の研究
537	Water is essential _to_ life.		水は生命に不可欠だ
538	a huge city		巨大な都市
539	a terrible accident		ひどい事故
540	practical English		実用的な英語

単語	意味	書きこみ①	書きこみ②	書きこみ③	No.
electricity [ilektrísəti]	電気				511
insect [ínsekt]	昆虫				512
web [wéb]	巣				513
storm [stɔ́ːrm]	嵐				514
plenty [plénti]	十分				515
agriculture [ǽɡrikʌltʃər]	農業				516
gene [dʒíːn]	遺伝子				517
evidence [évidəns]	証拠				518
consequence [kánsikwens]	結果				519
infant [ínfənt]	幼児				520
leisure [líːʒər]	暇				521
cell [sél]	細胞				522
talent [tǽlənt]	才能				523
advertising [ǽdvərtaiziŋ]	広告				524
extent [ikstént]	程度				525
garbage [ɡáːrbidʒ]	ゴミ				526
general [dʒénərəl]	一般の				527
various [véəriəs]	さまざまな				528
similar [símələr]	似ている				529
complete [kəmplíːt]	完全な				530
sharp [ʃáːrp]	急激な				531
expensive [ikspénsiv]	高価な				532
political [pəlítikəl]	政治的な				533
aware [əwéər]	気づいている				534
ancient [éinʃənt]	古代の				535
medical [médikəl]	医学の				536
essential [isénʃəl]	不可欠な				537
huge [hjúːdʒ]	巨大な				538
terrible [térəbl]	ひどい				539
practical [prǽktikəl]	実用的な				540

No.	英語フレーズ	フレーズ書きこみ	日本語フレーズ
541	the entire world		全世界
542	my favorite food		私のいちばん好きな食べ物
543	enjoy a comfortable life		快適な生活を楽しむ
544	a minor problem		小さい問題
545	a typical American family		典型的なアメリカの家族
546	an ideal place to live		生活するのに理想的な土地
547	the principal cities of Europe		ヨーロッパの主要な都市
548	the most appropriate word		最も適切な単語
549	an empty bottle		からのビン
550	rapid economic growth		急速な経済成長
551	a mental illness		精神の病
552	an excellent idea		すばらしいアイディア
553	when it's convenient *for* you		君の都合がいいときに
554	potential danger		潜在的な危険
555	financial support from the US		アメリカからの財政的援助
556	an enormous amount of damage		ばく大な額の損害
557	a rare stamp		珍しい切手
558	artificial intelligence		人工知能 (AI)
559	a tiny kitten		ちっちゃな子猫
560	spend considerable time		かなりの時間を費やす
561	Her skin is sensitive *to* sunlight.		彼女の肌は日光に敏感だ
562	high intellectual ability		高度な知的能力
563	Salty food makes you thirsty.		塩分の多い食事でのどが渇く
564	be polite to ladies		女性に対して礼儀正しい
565	accurate information		正確な情報
566	rude behavior		失礼な振る舞い
567	pay sufficient attention		十分な注意を払う
568	urban life		都会の暮らし
569	temporary loss of memory		一時的な記憶喪失
570	a primitive society		原始的な社会

単語	意味	書きこみ①	書きこみ②	書きこみ③	No.
entire [intáiər]	全体の				541
favorite [féivərət]	いちばん好きな				542
comfortable [kʌ́mfərtəbl]	快適な				543
minor [máinər]	小さい				544
typical [típikl]	典型的な				545
ideal [aidíːəl]	理想的な				546
principal [prínsəpl]	主要な				547
appropriate [əpróupriət]	適切な				548
empty [émpti]	からの				549
rapid [rǽpid]	急速な				550
mental [méntəl]	精神の				551
excellent [éksələnt]	すばらしい				552
convenient [kənvíːniənt]	都合がいい				553
potential [pəténʃəl]	潜在的な				554
financial [fainǽnʃəl]	財政的な				555
enormous [inɔ́ːrməs]	ばく大な				556
rare [réər]	珍しい				557
artificial [ɑːrtəfíʃəl]	人工の				558
tiny [táini]	ちっちゃな				559
considerable [kənsídərəbl]	かなりの				560
sensitive [sénsətiv]	敏感な				561
intellectual [intəléktʃuəl]	知的な				562
thirsty [θɔ́ːrsti]	のどが渇く				563
polite [pəláit]	礼儀正しい				564
accurate [ǽkjərət]	正確な				565
rude [rúːd]	失礼な				566
sufficient [səfíʃənt]	十分な				567
urban [ɔ́ːrbən]	都会の				568
temporary [témpəreri]	一時的な				569
primitive [prímətiv]	原始的な				570

No.	英語フレーズ	フレーズ書きこみ	日本語フレーズ
571	permanent teeth		永久歯
572	the care of elderly people		高齢者のケア
573	severe winter weather		厳しい冬の天候
574	a brief explanation		簡潔な説明
575	a mobile society		流動的な社会
576	the latest news from China		中国からの最新のニュース
577	military aid to Israel		イスラエルへの軍事的援助
578	strict rules		厳しい規則
579	a solid state		固体の状態
580	say stupid things		ばかなことを言う
581	biological weapons		生物兵器
582	Probably he won't come.		おそらく彼は来ないだろう
583	I hardly know Bill.		ビルのことはほとんど知らない
584	leave immediately after lunch		昼食後すぐに出発する
585	He eventually became president.		ついに彼は大統領になった
586	a frequently used word		しばしば使われる言葉
587	an extremely difficult problem		非常に難しい問題
588	gradually become colder		だんだん冷たくなる
589	instantly recognizable songs		すぐにそれとわかる歌
590	He is rich; nevertheless he is unhappy.		彼は金持ちだが、それにもかかわらず、不幸だ
591	He's kind; moreover, he's strong.		彼は親切で、その上強い
592	relatively few people		比較的少数の人々
593	an apparently simple question		一見簡単な問題
594	I will definitely not marry you.		絶対あなたとは結婚しない
595	largely because of the problem		主にその問題のせいで
596	The class is mostly Japanese.		クラスの大部分は日本人だ
597	approximately 10,000 years ago		およそ1万年前
598	stay overnight in his house		彼の家で一晩泊まる
599	accidentally discover an island		偶然島を発見する
600	He lost despite his efforts.		努力にもかかわらず彼は負けた

単語	意味	書きこみ①	書きこみ②	書きこみ③	No.
permanent [pə́ːrmənənt]	永久の				571
elderly [éldərli]	高齢の				572
severe [sivíər]	厳しい				573
brief [bríːf]	簡潔な				574
mobile [móubəl]	流動的な				575
latest [léitist]	最新の				576
military [míləteri]	軍事的な				577
strict [stríkt]	厳しい				578
solid [sálid]	固体の				579
stupid [stʲúːpid]	ばかな				580
biological [baiəládʒikəl]	生物の				581
probably [prábəbli]	おそらく				582
hardly [háːrdli]	ほとんど〜ない				583
immediately [imíːdiətli]	すぐに				584
eventually [ivéntʃuəli]	ついに				585
frequently [fríːkwəntli]	しばしば				586
extremely [ikstríːmli]	非常に				587
gradually [grǽdʒuəli]	だんだん				588
instantly [instəntli]	すぐに				589
nevertheless [nevərðəlés]	それにもかかわらず				590
moreover [mɔːróuvər]	その上				591
relatively [rélətivli]	比較的				592
apparently [əpǽrəntli]	一見				593
definitely [définətli]	絶対に				594
largely [láːrdʒli]	主に				595
mostly [móustli]	大部分は				596
approximately [əprǽksəmətli]	およそ				597
overnight [óuvərnáit]	一晩中				598
accidentally [ǽksidéntli]	偶然に				599
despite [dispáit]	前 〜にもかかわらず				600

⑺形容詞，⑻副詞・その他：本冊 p. 103 〜 107

1 Fundamental

Stage 2

Essential Stage

"*In the middle of difficulty lies opportunity*"
—— *Albert Einstein*

* * *

困難の中にチャンスがある。
—アルバート・アインシュタイン

No.	英語フレーズ	フレーズ書きこみ	日本語フレーズ
601	proceed straight ahead		まっすぐ前に進む
602	ensure the safety of drivers		ドライバーの安全を確保する
603	interpret the meaning of the word		その言葉の意味を解釈する
604	Some countries ceased _to_ exist.		いくつかの国は存在しなくなった
605	ban smoking in public places		公共の場の喫煙を禁ずる
606	obey the law		法に従う
607	eliminate the need for paper		紙の必要性をなくす
608	resist pressure from above		上からの圧力に抵抗する
609	accompany the president		大統領に同伴する
610	commit a crime		犯罪を犯す
611	pursue the American Dream		アメリカンドリームを追い求める
612	demonstrate _that_ it is impossible		それが不可能なことを示す
613	I bet you'll win.		きっと君は勝つと思う
614	ruin his life		彼の人生を破滅させる
615	threaten _to_ tell the police		警察に言うとおどす
616	a bookcase attached _to_ the wall		壁に取り付けられた本棚
617	reverse the positions		立場を逆転する
618	restrict freedom of speech		言論の自由を制限する
619	The body is composed _of_ cells.		体は細胞で構成されている
620	lean against the wall		壁にもたれる
621	substitute margarine _for_ butter		マーガリンをバターの代わりに用いる
622	trace human history		人類の歴史をたどる
623	interrupt their conversation		彼らの会話をじゃまする
624	confront a difficult problem		困難な問題に立ち向かう
625	This example illustrates his ability.		この例が彼の能力を示す
626	arrest him _for_ speeding		スピード違反で彼を逮捕する
627	stimulate the imagination		想像力を刺激する
628	assure you _that_ you will win		君が勝つことを保証する
629	consult a doctor for advice		医者に相談して助言を求める
630	feel too depressed to go out		憂鬱で出かける気がしない

単語	意味	書きこみ①	書きこみ②	書きこみ③	No.
proceed [prəsíːd]	進む				601
ensure [inʃúər]	～を確実にする				602
interpret [intə́ːrprit]	～を解釈する				603
cease to V [síːs]	Vしなくなる				604
ban [bǽn]	～を禁止する				605
obey [oubéi]	～に従う				606
eliminate [ilímineit]	～を除去する				607
resist [rizíst]	～に抵抗する				608
accompany [əkʌ́mpəni]	～に同伴する				609
commit [kəmít]	～を犯す				610
pursue [pərsjúː]	～を追求する				611
demonstrate [démənstreit]	～を明らかに示す				612
bet [bét]	きっと～だと思う				613
ruin [rúːin]	～を台無しにする				614
threaten [θrétn]	～を脅迫する				615
attach A to B [ətǽtʃ]	AをBにくっつける				616
reverse [rivə́ːrs]	～を反対にする				617
restrict [ristríkt]	～を制限する				618
compose [kəmpóuz]	～を組み立てる				619
lean [líːn]	寄りかかる				620
substitute [sʌ́bstətjuːt]	～を代わりに用いる				621
trace [tréis]	～の跡をたどる				622
interrupt [intərʌ́pt]	～を妨げる				623
confront [kənfrʌ́nt]	～の前に立ちふさがる				624
illustrate [íləstreit]	～を示す				625
arrest [ərést]	～を逮捕する				626
stimulate [stímjəleit]	～を刺激する				627
assure [əʃúər]	(～を) 保証する				628
consult [kənsʌ́lt]	～に相談する				629
depress [diprés]	～を憂鬱にさせる				630

2

Essential

No.	英語フレーズ	フレーズ書きこみ	日本語フレーズ
631	crash *into* the wall		壁に激突する
632	inspire him *to* write a poem		彼に詩を書く気を起こさせる
633	specialize *in* Chinese history		中国史を専攻する
634	cultivate plants		植物を栽培する
635	fulfill the promise		約束を果たす
636	transmit messages		メッセージを伝える
637	found a computer company		コンピュータ会社を設立する
638	Clap your hands as you sing.		歌いながら手をたたきなさい
639	burst *into* tears		急に泣き出す
640	bow *to* the queen		女王様におじぎする
641	dismiss the idea *as* nonsense		その考えをばからしいと無視する
642	how to breed animals		動物を繁殖させる方法
643	prohibit children *from* working		子供が働くのを禁じる
644	*be* obliged *to* pay the price		対価を支払わざるをえない
645	qualify *for* the position		その地位に適任である
646	invest money *in* a business		ビジネスにお金を投資する
647	grasp what he is saying		彼の言うことを理解する
648	The building collapsed.		建物が崩壊した
649	overlook the fact		事実を見逃す
650	accuse him *of* lying		彼がうそをついたと非難する
651	be frustrated by the lack of money		金がなくて欲求不満になる
652	deprive him *of* the chance		彼からチャンスを奪う
653	an astonishing memory		驚異的な記憶力
654	register a new car		新車を登録する
655	The fact corresponds *to* my theory.		その事実は私の理論と一致する
656	cast a shadow on the wall		壁に影を投げかける
657	attribute success *to* luck		成功は幸運のおかげだと思う
658	neglect human rights		人権を無視する
659	feed starving children		飢えた子どもたちに食事を与える
660	resolve disagreements		意見の不一致を解決する

⑴動詞：本冊 p. 115 〜 120

1回目 ／　2回目 ／　3回目 ／

単語	意味	書きこみ①	書きこみ②	書きこみ③	No.
crash [krǽʃ]	激突する				631
inspire [inspáiər]	〜を奮起させる				632
specialize in A [spéʃəlaiz]	Aを専門にする				633
cultivate [kʌ́ltəveit]	〜を栽培する				634
fulfill [fulfíl]	〜を果たす				635
transmit [trænsmít]	〜を送る				636
found [fáund]	〜を創立する				637
clap [klǽp]	〜をたたく				638
burst [bə́ːrst]	破裂する				639
bow [báu]	おじぎする				640
dismiss [dismís]	〜を無視する				641
breed [bríːd]	〜を繁殖させる				642
prohibit [prouhíbət]	〜を禁じる				643
oblige [əbláidʒ]	〜に強いる				644
qualify for A [kwɑ́ləfai]	Aに適任である				645
invest [invést]	投資する				646
grasp [grǽsp]	〜を理解する				647
collapse [kəlǽps]	崩壊する				648
overlook [ouvərlúk]	〜を見落とす				649
accuse [əkjúːz]	〜を非難する				650
frustrate [frʌ́streit]	〜を欲求不満にさせる				651
deprive A of B [dipráiv]	AからBを奪う				652
astonish [əstɑ́niʃ]	〜を驚嘆させる				653
register [rédʒistər]	〜を登録する				654
correspond [kɔrəspɑ́nd]	一致する				655
cast [kǽst]	〜を投げる				656
attribute A to B [ətríbjuːt] 名 [ǽtribjuːt]	AをBのおかげだと思う				657
neglect [niglékt]	〜を無視する				658
starve [stɑ́ːrv]	飢える				659
resolve [rizɑ́lv]	〜を解決する				660

2
Essential

No.	英語フレーズ	フレーズ書きこみ	日本語フレーズ
661	impose rules _on_ students		学生に規則を押しつける
662	convert sunlight _into_ electricity		太陽の光を電気に転換する
663	The noise scares him.		その音が彼をおびえさせる
664	Cars constitute 10% of exports.		車が輸出の10%を占める
665	_be_ appointed _to_ an important post		重要なポストに任命される
666	What does her smile imply?		彼女の微笑みは何を意味するのか
667	assign work _to_ each member		各メンバーに仕事を割り当てる
668	nod and say "yes"		うなずいて「はい」と言う
669	_be_ elected president		大統領に選ばれる
670	He was transferred _to_ Osaka.		彼は大阪に転動した
671	rob the bank _of_ $50,000		銀行から5万ドル奪う
672	capture wild animals		野生動物を捕らえる
673	undertake the work		仕事を引き受ける
674	save a drowning child		おぼれている子供を救う
675	split into two groups		2つのグループに分裂する
676	resort _to_ violence		暴力に訴える
677	descend to the ground		地面に降りる
678	irritating noise		いらいらさせる騒音
679	pronounce the word correctly		正確にその単語を発音する
680	The car is equipped _with_ AI.		その車はAIが装備されている
681	cheat consumers		消費者をだます
682	A new problem has emerged.		新たな問題が出現した
683	He devoted _himself to_ his work.		彼は仕事に身をささげた
684	Time heals all wounds.		時はすべての傷をいやす
685	urge him _to_ go home		帰宅するよう彼を説得する
686	envy the rich		金持ちをうらやむ
687	chase the car		その車を追跡する
688	prompt him to speak		彼に話をするよう促す
689	withdraw my hand		手を引っ込める
690	how to detect lies		うそを発見する方法

単語	意味	書きこみ①	書きこみ②	書きこみ③	No.
impose A on B [impóuz]	AをBに課す				661
convert [kənvə́ːrt]	〜を転換する				662
scare [skéər]	〜をおびえさせる				663
constitute [kánstətjuːt]	〜を構成する				664
appoint [əpɔ́int]	〜を任命する				665
imply [implái]	〜を意味する				666
assign [əsáin]	〜を割り当てる				667
nod [nád]	うなずく				668
elect [ilékt]	〜を選挙で選ぶ				669
transfer [trænsfə́ːr]	〜を移す				670
rob A of B [ráb]	AからBを奪う				671
capture [kǽptʃər]	〜を捕らえる				672
undertake [ʌndərtéik]	〜を引き受ける				673
drown [dráun]	おぼれ死ぬ				674
split [splít]	〜を割る				675
resort to A [rizɔ́ːrt]	Aに訴える				676
descend [disénd]	下る				677
irritate [íriteit]	〜をいらだたせる				678
pronounce [prənáuns]	〜を発音する				679
equip [ikwíp]	〜を装備させる				680
cheat [tʃíːt]	いかさまをする				681
emerge [imə́ːrdʒ]	現れる				682
devote [divóut]	〜をささげる				683
heal [híːl]	〜を治す				684
urge [ə́ːrdʒ]	〜に強く迫る				685
envy [énvi]	〜をうらやむ				686
chase [tʃéis]	〜を追いかける				687
prompt [prámpt]	〜を促す				688
withdraw [wiðdrɔ́ː]	〜を引っ込める				689
detect [ditékt]	〜を探知する				690

2

Essential

No.	英語フレーズ	フレーズ書きこみ	日本語フレーズ
691	interfere _with_ his work		彼の仕事をじゃまする
692	You must be kidding.		冗談でしょう
693	launch a space shuttle		スペースシャトルを発射する
694	an endangered species		絶滅危惧種
695	foster creativity		創造性を養う
696	His power diminished.		彼の力は衰えた
697	spill coffee on the keyboard		キーボードにコーヒーをこぼす
698	be infected _with_ the virus		ウイルスに感染している
699	stem _from_ an ancient tradition		古い伝統に由来する
700	tap her on the shoulder		彼女の肩を軽くたたく
701	embrace a new idea		新しい考えを受け入れる
702	the proportion of boys _to_ girls		男子と女子の比率
703	sign a contract _with_ Google		グーグルとの契約にサインする
704	have chest pains		胸が痛む
705	discover treasure		財宝を発見する
706	the Tokyo stock market		東京株式市場
707	public facilities		公共施設
708	a large sum of money		多額のお金
709	a man of high rank		高い地位の人
710	a modern democracy		近代民主国家
711	an emergency room		救急治療室
712	a protest _against_ war		戦争に対する抗議
713	immigrants from Mexico		メキシコからの移民
714	a vehicle for communication		意思伝達の手段
715	a healthy daily routine		健康的ないつもの日課
716	write really good stuff		本当によいものを書く
717	sit in the front row		最前列に座る
718	your online profile		君のオンラインのプロフィール
719	leave home _at_ dawn		夜明けに家を出る
720	social welfare		社会福祉

単語	意味	書きこみ①	書きこみ②	書きこみ③	No.
interfere with A [ìntərfíər]	Aをじゃまする				691
kid [kíd]	冗談を言う				692
launch [lɔ́:ntʃ]	〜を打ち上げる				693
endanger [endéindʒər]	〜を危険にさらす				694
foster [fɔ́(:)stər]	〜を促進する				695
diminish [dimíniʃ]	減少する				696
spill [spíl]	〜をこぼす				697
infect [infékt]	〜に感染する				698
stem from A [stém]	Aから生じる				699
tap [tǽp]	〜を軽くたたく				700
embrace [imbréis]	〜を受け入れる				701
proportion [prəpɔ́:rʃən]	比率				702
contract [kɑ́ntrækt]　動 [- ´]	契約				703
chest [tʃést]	胸				704
treasure [tréʒər]	財宝				705
stock [stɑ́k]	株（式）				706
facility [fəsíləti]	設備				707
sum [sʌ́m]	金額				708
rank [rǽŋk]	地位				709
democracy [dimɑ́krəsi]	民主主義				710
emergency [imɔ́:rdʒənsi]	緊急事態				711
protest [próutest]　動 [prətést]	抗議				712
immigrant [ímigrənt]	移民				713
vehicle [ví:əkl]	車				714
routine [ru:tí:n]	決まりきった仕事				715
stuff [stʌ́f]	物				716
row [róu]	列				717
profile [próufail]	プロフィール				718
dawn [dɔ́:n]	夜明け				719
welfare [wélfeər]	福祉				720

No.	英語フレーズ	フレーズ書きこみ	日本語フレーズ
721	see life *from* a new perspective		新しい見方で人生を考える
722	his enthusiasm *for* soccer		彼のサッカーに対する情熱
723	have faith *in* technology		技術を信頼する
724	a well-paid occupation		給料のよい職業
725	a witness to the accident		事故の目撃者
726	the kingdom of Denmark		デンマーク王国
727	There's no English equivalent *to* haiku.		俳句に相当するものは英語にない
728	achieve the objective		目標を達成する
729	put the plates in a pile		皿を積み重ねて置く
730	find shelter *from* the cold		寒さから逃れる場所を見つける
731	trial and error		試行錯誤
732	It's a great honor to work here.		ここで働けるのは大変名誉です
733	defend a territory		なわ張りを守る
734	a window frame		窓わく
735	cross the Russian border		ロシア国境を越える
736	according to official statistics		公式の統計によると
737	a private enterprise		民間企業
738	the meaning *in* this context		この文脈における意味
739	carry a heavy load		重い荷物を運ぶ
740	world grain production		世界の穀物生産高
741	a review of the law		その法律の再検討
742	prejudice against women		女性に対する偏見
743	put a strain *on* the heart		心臓に負担をかける
744	fall into a trap		わなにはまる
745	have a quick temper		すぐかっとなる気性である
746	a black slave		黒人の奴隷
747	a knife wound		ナイフの傷
748	an increase in the divorce rate		離婚率の増加
749	the beauty of the tune		その曲の美しさ
750	Summer is *at* its height.		夏真っ盛りだ

単語	意味	書きこみ①	書きこみ②	書きこみ③	No.
perspective [pərspéktiv]	見方				721
enthusiasm [inθjú:ziæzm]	熱意				722
faith [féiθ]	信頼				723
occupation [ɑkjəpéiʃən]	職業				724
witness [wítnəs]	証人				725
kingdom [kíŋdəm]	王国				726
equivalent [ikwívələnt]	同等のもの				727
objective [əbdʒéktiv]	目的				728
pile [páil]	積み重ね				729
shelter [ʃéltər]	避難 (所)				730
trial [tráiəl]	試み				731
honor [ɑ́nər]	名誉				732
territory [térətɔ:ri]	領土				733
frame [fréim]	わく				734
border [bɔ́:rdər]	国境地帯				735
statistics [stətístiks]	統計 (学)				736
enterprise [éntərpraiz]	企業				737
context [kántekst]	文脈				738
load [lóud]	荷物				739
grain [gréin]	穀物				740
review [rivjú:]	再検討				741
prejudice [prédʒədəs]	偏見				742
strain [stréin]	負担				743
trap [trǽp]	わな				744
temper [témpər]	気性				745
slave [sléiv]	奴隷				746
wound [wú:nd]	傷				747
divorce [divɔ́:rs]	離婚				748
tune [tjú:n]	曲				749
height [háit]	高さ				750

2
Essential

No.	英語フレーズ	フレーズ書きこみ	日本語フレーズ
751	the science faculty		理学部
752	the average *life* span		平均寿命
753	the moral dimension of science		科学の道徳的側面
754	the latest version of the software		そのソフトの最新版
755	have no parallel in history		歴史上匹敵するものがない
756	the moon rising *on* the horizon		地平線に昇る月
757	friends and acquaintances		友人と知人
758	become a burden *on* society		社会の重荷になる
759	the scientific basis of his theory		彼の理論の科学的根拠
760	poison gas		毒ガス
761	the Constitution of Japan		日本国憲法
762	business administration		企業の経営
763	a city full of charm		魅力にあふれた都市
764	sense organs		感覚器官
765	the prey of the lion		ライオンのえじき
766	a *joint* venture with Taiwan		台湾との共同事業
767	carry out a dangerous mission		危険な任務を果たす
768	an inquiry into the accident		事故に関する調査
769	the Academy Award *for* Best Picture		アカデミー最優秀作品賞
770	a long strip of paper		長い紙切れ
771	be in economic distress		経済的苦難におちいる
772	increase blood circulation		血液の循環を高める
773	keep the beer in the shade		ビールを日陰に置く
774	a stereotype of Americans		アメリカ人に関する型にはまったイメージ
775	a lawyer and his client		弁護士とその依頼人
776	the factory's output		その工場の生産高
777	praise the Lord		神をたたえる
778	follow social conventions		社会の慣習に従う
779	discover a gold mine		金鉱を発見する
780	a traditional Japanese craft		日本の伝統工芸

単語	意味	書きこみ①	書きこみ②	書きこみ③	No.
faculty [fǽkəlti]	学部				751
span [spǽn]	期間				752
dimension [diménʃən]	側面				753
version [və́ːrʒən]	型				754
parallel [pǽrəlel]	類似（物）				755
horizon [həráizn]	地平線				756
acquaintance [əkwéintəns]	知人				757
burden [bə́ːrdn]	重荷				758
basis [béisis]	基礎				759
poison [pɔ́izn]	毒				760
constitution [kɑnstətúːʃən]	憲法				761
administration [ədministréiʃən]	経営				762
charm [tʃɑ́ːrm]	魅力				763
organ [ɔ́ːrgən]	臓器				764
prey [préi]	獲物				765
venture [véntʃər]	冒険的事業				766
mission [míʃən]	使命				767
inquiry [inkwáiəri]	調査				768
award [əwɔ́ːrd]	賞				769
strip [stríp]	細長い一片				770
distress [distrés]	苦しみ				771
circulation [sə̀ːrkjuléiʃən]	循環				772
shade [ʃéid]	陰				773
stereotype [stériətaip]	典型的なイメージ				774
client [kláiənt]	依頼人				775
output [áutput]	生産高				776
lord [lɔ́ːrd]	神				777
convention [kənvénʃən]	慣習				778
mine [máin]	鉱山				779
craft [krǽft]	工芸				780

2
Essential

No.	英語フレーズ	フレーズ書きこみ	日本語フレーズ
781	the core *of* the problem		問題の核心
782	have a stroke		脳卒中になる
783	America's last frontier		アメリカ最後の辺境
784	He's popular with his peers.		彼は同僚に人気だ
785	blood vessels		血管
786	people with disabilities		障害を持つ人々
787	zero gravity in space		宇宙の無重力状態
788	a question of medical ethics		医学の倫理の問題
789	a railroad terminal		鉄道の終点
790	swim against the tide		潮流に逆らって泳ぐ
791	child abuse		児童虐待
792	feel guilty about leaving him		彼を捨てたことに罪の意識を感じる
793	be vital *to* human health		人の健康にきわめて重要だ
794	his fellow workers		彼の仕事仲間
795	contemporary Japanese society		現代の日本社会
796	his annual income		彼の年収
797	become accustomed *to* driv*ing*		車の運転に慣れる
798	steady economic growth		着実な経済成長
799	very dull work		とても退屈な仕事
800	I'm keen *to* talk to him.		私は彼と話をしたい
801	wear loose clothes		ゆったりとした服を着る
802	the delicate balance of nature		自然界の微妙なバランス
803	internal medicine		内科
804	wear casual clothes		気楽な服装をする
805	mature adults		成熟した大人
806	give a concrete example		具体的な例をあげる
807	How awful!		なんてひどい!
808	be exhausted from overwork		過労で疲れ切っている
809	part of an overall plan		全体的な計画の一部
810	tight jeans		きついジーンズ

単語	意味	書きこみ①	書きこみ②	書きこみ③	No.
core [kɔ́ːr]	中心				781
stroke [stróuk]	脳卒中				782
frontier [frʌ́ntíər]	国境				783
peer [píər]	同僚				784
vessel [vésl]	血管				785
disability [dìsəbíləti]	障害				786
gravity [grǽvəti]	重力				787
ethic [éθik]	倫理(学)				788
terminal [tə́ːrmənl]	終点				789
tide [táid]	潮流				790
abuse [əbjúːs]　動 [əbjúːz]	虐待				791
guilty [gílti]	有罪の				792
vital [váitl]	きわめて重要な				793
fellow [félou]	仲間の				794
contemporary [kəntémpəreri]	現代の				795
annual [ǽnjuəl]	年に1度の				796
accustomed [əkʌ́stəmd]	慣れた				797
steady [stédi]	しっかりした				798
dull [dʌ́l]	退屈させる				799
keen [kíːn]	熱望して				800
loose [lúːs]	ゆるい				801
delicate [délikət]	繊細な				802
internal [intə́ːrnəl]	内部の				803
casual [kǽʒuəl]	形式ばらない				804
mature [mətúər]	成熟した				805
concrete [kánkriːt]	具体的な				806
awful [ɔ́ːfl]	ひどい				807
exhausted [igzɔ́ːstid]	疲れ切っている				808
overall [óuvərɔːl]	全面的な				809
tight [táit]	引き締まった				810

2

Essential

No.	英語フレーズ	フレーズ書きこみ	日本語フレーズ
811	the prime cause		主要な原因
812	a genuine interest in science		科学に対する真の関心
813	a modest dress		控えめな服装
814	an intimate relationship		親密な関係
815	minimum effort		最小の努力
816	sophisticated computer technology		高度なコンピュータ技術
817	I have a dog and a cat. *The* latter is bigger.		犬と猫を飼っているが，後者の方が大きい
818	a bitter experience		苦い経験
819	expressions peculiar *to* English		英語特有の表現
820	a passive attitude		消極的な態度
821	different ethnic groups		異なる民族集団
822	a person of noble birth		高貴な生まれの人
823	make a vain effort		むだな努力をする
824	blame innocent people		罪の無い人々を責める
825	the underlying cause		根本的な原因
826	an alien species		外来種
827	be relevant *to* the question		その問題に関係がある
828	I *am* inclined *to* believe him.		彼の言葉を信じたい気がする
829	an awkward silence		気まずい沈黙
830	That's a brilliant idea!		それはすばらしいアイディアだ!
831	a desperate attempt		必死の試み
832	a refreshing drink		さわやかな飲み物
833	I'm thrilled to hear your voice.		君の声が聞けてとてもうれしい
834	her inner self		彼女の内なる自分
835	be consistent *with* the theory		理論と一致する
836	be written in plain English		平易な英語で書かれている
837	have vivid memories		鮮やかな思い出がある
838	a miserable life		惨めな生活
839	a substantial number of people		相当な数の人々
840	She is very fond *of* reading.		彼女は読書が大好きだ

単語	意味	書きこみ①	書きこみ②	書きこみ③	No.
prime [práim]	最も重要な				811
genuine [dʒénjuin]	本物の				812
modest [mádəst]	控えめな				813
intimate [íntəmət]	親密な				814
minimum [míniməm]	最小限の				815
sophisticated [səfístikeitid]	高度な				816
latter [lǽtər]	後者の				817
bitter [bítər]	苦い				818
peculiar [pikjúːliər]	独特の				819
passive [pǽsiv]	受動的な				820
ethnic [éθnik]	民族的な				821
noble [nóubl]	高貴な				822
vain [véin]	むだな				823
innocent [ínəsənt]	無罪の				824
underlying [ʌndərláiiŋ]	根本的な				825
alien [éiljən]	外国（人）の				826
relevant [réləvənt]	関連のある				827
be inclined to V [inkláind]	Vしたい気がする				828
awkward [ɔ́ːkwərd]	気まずい				829
brilliant [bríljənt]	すばらしい				830
desperate [déspərət]	必死の				831
refreshing [rifréʃiŋ]	さわやかな				832
thrilled [θríld]	とてもうれしい				833
inner [ínər]	内側の				834
consistent [kənsístənt]	矛盾のない				835
plain [pléin]	明白な				836
vivid [vívid]	鮮やかな				837
miserable [mízərəbl]	惨めな				838
substantial [səbstǽnʃəl]	相当な				839
be fond of A [fánd]	Aが好きだ				840

2

Essential

No.	英語フレーズ	フレーズ書きこみ	日本語フレーズ
841	True or false?		正しいかまちがいか
842	a lazy student		怠惰な学生
843	precisely at noon		ちょうど正午に
844	She was cooking. Meanwhile, I was drinking.		彼女は料理をしていた。その間, 私は酒を飲んでいた。
845	disappear altogether		完全に消滅する
846	Have you seen him lately?		最近彼に会いましたか
847	barely survive the war		かろうじて戦争を生き延びる
848	I could scarcely believe it.		ほとんど信じられなかった
849	You're an adult, so act accordingly.		君は大人なのだからそれ相応に行動しなさい
850	deliberately ignore him		彼をわざと無視する
851	beneath the surface of the water		水面下で
852	The British say "lift," whereas Americans say "elevator."		イギリス人は「リフト」と言うが, アメリカ人は「エレベータ」と言う
853	declare independence from Britain		イギリスからの独立を宣言する
854	alter the pattern of behavior		行動パターンを変える
855	Problems arise *from* carelessness.		不注意から問題が生じる
856	transform food *into* energy		食べ物をエネルギーに変える
857	defeat the champion		チャンピオンを打ち負かす
858	investigate the cause of the failure		失敗の原因を調査する
859	distinguish a lie *from* the truth		うそと真実を見分ける
860	bury treasure		宝物を埋める
861	cope *with* problems		問題にうまく対処する
862	This problem often occurs.		この問題はしばしば起こる
863	accomplish the difficult task		困難な仕事をやりとげる
864	Don't hesitate *to* ask questions.		質問するのをためらうな
865	endure great pain		ひどい苦痛に耐える
866	conclude that he is OK		彼は大丈夫だと結論づける
867	guarantee your success		君の成功を保証する
868	dominate the world economy		世界経済を支配する
869	confirm Darwin's theory		ダーウィンの理論を裏づける
870	greet people with a smile		笑顔で人にあいさつする

単語	意味	書きこみ①	書きこみ②	書きこみ③	No.
false [fɔ́:ls]	まちがいの				841
lazy [léizi]	怠惰な				842
precisely [prisáisli]	正確に				843
meanwhile [mí:nhwail]	その間に				844
altogether [ɔ:ltəgéðər]	完全に				845
lately [léitli]	最近				846
barely [béərli]	かろうじて				847
scarcely [skéərsli]	ほとんど〜ない				848
accordingly [əkɔ́:rdiŋli]	それ相応に				849
deliberately [dilíbərətli]	わざと				850
beneath [biní:θ]	前 〜の下で				851
whereas [hweərǽz]	接 〜だが一方				852
declare [dikléər]	〜を宣言する				853
alter [ɔ́:ltər]	〜を変える				854
arise [əráiz]	生じる				855
transform [trænsfɔ́:rm]	変える				856
defeat [difí:t]	〜を打ち負かす				857
investigate [invéstəgeit]	〜を調査する				858
distinguish [distíŋgwiʃ]	〜を見分ける				859
bury [béri]	〜を埋める				860
cope [kóup]	うまく対処する				861
occur [əkɔ́:r]	起こる				862
accomplish [əkámpliʃ]	〜をやりとげる				863
hesitate [héziteit]	ためらう				864
endure [endʒúər]	〜に耐える				865
conclude [kənklú:d]	結論づける				866
guarantee [gærəntí:]	〜を保証する				867
dominate [dáməneit]	〜を支配する				868
confirm [kənfɔ́:rm]	〜を裏づける				869
greet [grí:t]	〜にあいさつする				870

2 Essential

No.	英語フレーズ	フレーズ書きこみ	日本語フレーズ
871 ☐	entertain the audience		観客を楽しませる
872 ☐	defend ourselves *against* attack		攻撃から自分たちを守る
873 ☐	forbid him *to* go out		彼の外出を禁じる
874 ☐	broadcast the concert live		生でコンサートを放送する
875 ☐	sacrifice everything for love		愛のためすべてを犠牲にする
876 ☐	punish him *for* the crime		その罪で彼を罰する
877 ☐	glance *at* the clock		時計をちらりと見る
878 ☐	retain the world title		世界タイトルを保持する
879 ☐	calculate the cost		コストを計算する
880 ☐	leave a sinking ship		沈む船から逃げる
881 ☐	rescue a man from a fire		火事で人を救助する
882 ☐	beg him *to* come back		彼に帰って来てと乞う
883 ☐	define a day *as* twenty-four hours		1日を24時間と定義する
884 ☐	It is easy to deceive people.		人をだますのは簡単だ
885 ☐	convey information		情報を伝える
886 ☐	energy to sustain life		生命を維持するためのエネルギー
887 ☐	purchase the land		その土地を購入する
888 ☐	Memories of the war fade *away*.		戦争の記憶が薄れる
889 ☐	regulate traffic		交通を規制する
890 ☐	distribute food equally		平等に食料を分配する
891 ☐	enhance the quality of life		生活の質を向上させる
892 ☐	chat *with* friends		友達とおしゃべりする
893 ☐	Demand exceeds supply.		需要が供給を超える
894 ☐	wipe the table		テーブルをふく
895 ☐	cooperate *with* each other		お互いに協力する
896 ☐	inherit genes *from* our parents		親から遺伝子を受け継ぐ
897 ☐	unite the Arab world		アラブ世界を団結させる
898 ☐	Look before you leap.		跳ぶ前によく見よ
899 ☐	exaggerate the size of the fish		魚の大きさを誇張する
900 ☐	conquer the world		世界を征服する

(5)動詞：本冊 p. 158 〜 162

単語	意味	書きこみ①	書きこみ②	書きこみ③	No.
entertain [entərtéin]	〜を楽しませる				871
defend [difénd]	〜を守る				872
forbid [fərbíd]	〜を禁じる				873
broadcast [brɔ́:dkæst]	〜を放送する				874
sacrifice [sǽkrəfais]	〜を犠牲にする				875
punish [pʌ́niʃ]	〜を罰する				876
glance [glǽns]	ちらりと見る				877
retain [ritéin]	〜を保持する				878
calculate [kǽlkjəleit]	〜を計算する				879
sink [síŋk]	沈む				880
rescue [réskju:]	〜を救助する				881
beg [bég]	〜と乞う				882
define [difáin]	定義する				883
deceive [disí:v]	〜をだます				884
convey [kənvéi]	〜を伝える				885
sustain [səstéin]	〜を維持する				886
purchase [pə́:rtʃəs]	〜を購入する				887
fade [féid]	薄れる				888
regulate [régjəleit]	〜を規制する				889
distribute [distríbju:t]	〜を分配する				890
enhance [inhǽns]	〜を向上させる				891
chat [tʃǽt]	おしゃべりする				892
exceed [iksí:d]	〜を超える				893
wipe [wáip]	〜をふく				894
cooperate [kouápəreit]	協力する				895
inherit [inhérit]	〜を受け継ぐ				896
unite [ju:náit]	〜を団結させる				897
leap [lí:p]	跳ぶ				898
exaggerate [igzǽdʒəreit]	〜を誇張する				899
conquer [káŋkər]	〜を征服する				900

2 Essential

No.	英語フレーズ	フレーズ書きこみ	日本語フレーズ
901	The snow will melt soon.		雪は間もなく溶けるだろう
902	invade Poland		ポーランドに侵入する
903	modify the plan		計画を修正する
904	scatter toys on the floor		床におもちゃをばらまく
905	undergo great changes		大きな変化を経験する
906	evaluate online information		オンライン情報を評価する
907	bend down to pick up the can		カンを拾おうと身をかがめる
908	The word derives *from* Latin.		その単語はラテン語に由来する
909	a girl screaming for help		助けを求め悲鳴をあげる少女
910	gaze *at* the stars		星を見つめる
911	pray for a sick child		病気の子供のために祈る
912	polish the shoes		靴を磨く
913	classify man *as* an animal		人間を動物として分類する
914	assert *that* it is impossible		それは不可能だと主張する
915	grab him by the arm		彼の腕をつかむ
916	fold a piece of paper		紙を折りたたむ
917	sweep the floor		床を掃く
918	whisper in her ear		彼女の耳にささやく
919	imitate human behavior		人間の行動をまねる
920	stop and stare *at* her		立ち止まって彼女をじっと見る
921	emphasize the importance of health		健康の大切さを強調する
922	*get* rid *of* stress		ストレスを取り除く
923	pour wine into the glass		グラスにワインを注ぐ
924	vanish from sight		視界から消える
925	restore the old building		古い建物を修復する
926	deserve *to be* punished		罰を受けて当然だ
927	a space science laboratory		宇宙科学研究所
928	an international conference		国際会議
929	cross the American continent		アメリカ大陸を横断する
930	national health insurance		国民健康保険

⑸動詞, ⑹名詞：本冊 p. 162 ～ 166

2 Essential

単語	意味	書きこみ①	書きこみ②	書きこみ③	No.
melt [mélt]	溶ける				901
invade [invéid]	～に侵入する				902
modify [mádifai]	～を修正する				903
scatter [skǽtər]	～をばらまく				904
undergo [ʌndərgóu]	～を経験する				905
evaluate [ivǽljueit]	～を評価する				906
bend [bénd]	身をかがめる				907
derive [diráiv]	由来する				908
scream [skrí:m]	悲鳴をあげる				909
gaze [géiz]	見つめる				910
pray [préi]	祈る				911
polish [páliʃ]	～を磨く				912
classify [klǽsifai]	分類する				913
assert [əsə́ːrt]	～と主張する				914
grab [grǽb]	～をつかむ				915
fold [fóuld]	～を折りたたむ				916
sweep [swí:p]	～を掃く				917
whisper [hwíspər]	ささやく				918
imitate [íməteit]	～をまねる				919
stare [stéər]	じっと見る				920
emphasize [émfəsaiz]	～を強調する				921
rid [ríd]	～を取り除く				922
pour [pɔ́ːr]	～を注ぐ				923
vanish [vǽniʃ]	消える				924
restore [ristɔ́ːr]	～を修復する				925
deserve [dizə́ːrv]	当然だ				926
laboratory [lǽbərətɔːri]	研究所				927
conference [kánfərəns]	会議				928
continent [kántinənt]	大陸				929
insurance [inʃúərəns]	保険				930

No.	英語フレーズ	フレーズ書きこみ	日本語フレーズ
931 ☐	the crew of the space shuttle		スペースシャトルの乗組員たち
932 ☐	live in poverty		貧乏な生活をする
933 ☐	water shortage		水不足
934 ☐	international affairs		国際情勢
935 ☐	the only exception *to* the rule		その規則の唯一の例外
936 ☐	work for *low* wages		安い賃金で働く
937 ☐	knowledge and wisdom		知識と知恵
938 ☐	pay taxes *on* the land		その土地にかかる税金を払う
939 ☐	human evolution		人類の進化
940 ☐	the language barrier		言葉の壁
941 ☐	fall into the same category		同じ範ちゅうに属する
942 ☐	the family as a social unit		社会の単位としての家族
943 ☐	the restaurant's reputation		そのレストランの評判
944 ☐	the virtue of hard work		勤勉の美徳
945 ☐	have the courage *to* tell the truth		真実を話す勇気を持つ
946 ☐	feel sympathy *for* the victim		犠牲者に同情する
947 ☐	a labor union		労働組合
948 ☐	Western civilization		西洋文明
949 ☐	a 10,000-volume library		蔵書1万冊の図書館
950 ☐	cherry blossoms		サクラの花
951 ☐	the beginning of a new era		新しい時代の始まり
952 ☐	*settle* international disputes		国際紛争を解決する
953 ☐	the tourism industry in Japan		日本の観光産業
954 ☐	the history of mankind		人類の歴史
955 ☐	mass murder		大量殺人
956 ☐	landscape painting		風景画
957 ☐	reach the final destination		最終目的地に着く
958 ☐	tell a *fairy* tale		おとぎ話をする
959 ☐	political reform		政治改革
960 ☐	muscles and bones		筋肉と骨

単語	意味	書きこみ①	書きこみ②	書きこみ③	No.
crew [krúː]	乗組員たち				931
poverty [pávərti]	貧乏				932
shortage [ʃɔ́ːrtidʒ]	不足				933
affair [əféər]	情勢				934
exception [iksépʃən]	例外				935
wage [wéidʒ]	賃金				936
wisdom [wízdəm]	知恵				937
tax [tǽks]	税金				938
evolution [evəljúːʃən]	進化				939
barrier [bǽriər]	壁				940
category [kǽtəgɔːri]	範ちゅう				941
unit [júːnit]	単位				942
reputation [repjutéiʃən]	評判				943
virtue [vɔ́ːrtʃuː]	美徳				944
courage [kɔ́ːridʒ]	勇気				945
sympathy [símpəθi]	同情				946
union [júːnjən]	組合				947
civilization [sivəlizéiʃən]	文明				948
volume [válju(ː)m]	冊				949
blossom [blásəm]	花				950
era [íːrə]	時代				951
dispute [dispjúːt]	紛争				952
tourism [túərizm]	観光				953
mankind [mænkáind]	人類				954
murder [mɔ́ːrdər]	殺人				955
landscape [lǽndskeip]	風景				956
destination [destinéiʃən]	目的地				957
tale [téil]	話				958
reform [rifɔ́ːrm]	改革				959
muscle [mʌ́sl]	筋肉				960

2
Essential

No.	英語フレーズ	フレーズ書きこみ	日本語フレーズ
961	future prospects		将来の見通し
962	run a large corporation		大企業を経営する
963	a former British colony		元イギリスの植民地
964	a quarrel _with_ my wife		妻との口論
965	an intellectual profession		知的職業
966	unique aspects _of_ Japanese culture		日本文化のユニークな側面
967	a three-minute pause		3分間の休止
968	the conflict _between_ the two sides		その両者間の対立
969	white privilege		白人の特権
970	economic prosperity		経済的繁栄
971	a musical genius		音楽の天才
972	plant pumpkin seeds		カボチャの種をまく
973	symptoms of a cold		カゼの症状
974	his greatest merit		彼の最大の長所
975	destroy the ozone layer		オゾン層を破壊する
976	a clue _to_ the mystery		その謎を解く手がかり
977	_under_ any circumstances		いかなる状況においても
978	the city's business district		その都市の商業地区
979	spend two years in prison		刑務所で2年過ごす
980	my traveling companion		私の旅行仲間
981	chief executive officer		最高経営責任者 (CEO)
982	a strong sense of justice		強い正義感
983	the check-in procedure		チェックインの手続き
984	the sun's rays		太陽光線
985	go to heaven		天国に昇る
986	lead a life of luxury		ぜいたくな生活を送る
987	oxygen in the air		空気中の酸素
988	lack of funds		資金不足
989	the theme of the book		その本の主題
990	the boundary _between_ two countries		二国間の境界

単語	意味	書きこみ①	書きこみ②	書きこみ③	No.
prospect [práspekt]	見通し				961
corporation [kɔːrpəréiʃən]	企業				962
colony [káləni]	植民地				963
quarrel [kwɔ́(ː)rəl]	口論				964
profession [prəféʃən]	職業				965
aspect [æspekt]	側面				966
pause [pɔ́ːz]	休止				967
conflict [kánflikt] 動 [kənflíkt]	対立				968
privilege [prívilidʒ]	特権				969
prosperity [prɑspérəti]	繁栄				970
genius [dʒíːnjəs]	天才				971
seed [síːd]	種				972
symptom [símptəm]	症状				973
merit [mérit]	長所				974
layer [léiər]	層				975
clue [klúː]	手がかり				976
circumstances [sɔ́ːrkəmstænsiz]	状況				977
district [dístrikt]	地区				978
prison [prízn]	刑務所				979
companion [kəmpǽnjən]	仲間				980
executive [igzékjətiv]	執行責任者				981
justice [dʒʌ́stis]	正義				982
procedure [prəsíːdʒər]	手続き				983
ray [réi]	光線				984
heaven [hévən]	天国				985
luxury [lʌ́gʒəri]	ぜいたく				986
oxygen [áksidʒən]	酸素				987
fund [fʌ́nd]	資金				988
theme [θíːm]	主題				989
boundary [báundəri]	境界				990

No.	英語フレーズ	フレーズ書きこみ	日本語フレーズ
991	his ambition *to* be a writer		作家になりたいという彼の熱望
992	the *weather* forecast		天気予報
993	study social psychology		社会心理学を研究する
994	do hard labor		重労働を行う
995	the International Olympic Committee		国際オリンピック委員会 (IOC)
996	a physician at the hospital		その病院の医者
997	his philosophy of life		彼の人生哲学
998	a deep affection *for* animals		動物への深い愛情
999	a candidate *for* President		大統領候補
1000	an atomic bomb		原子爆弾
1001	give top priority to safety		安全を最優先する
1002	an obstacle *to* communication		コミュニケーションの障害
1003	have no appetite		食欲がない
1004	relieve tension		緊張を緩和する
1005	a Native American tribe		アメリカ先住民の部族
1006	cut the defense budget		防衛予算を削減する
1007	thc campaign *to* promotc tourism		観光を促進する運動
1008	joy and sorrow		喜びと悲しみ
1009	a communications satellite		通信衛星
1010	a deep insight *into* life		人生に対する深い洞察
1011	have a bad cough		ひどいせきが出る
1012	decide the fate of the world		世界の運命を決定する
1013	a training scheme for pilots		パイロットの訓練計画
1014	an insult to women		女性に対する侮辱
1015	the inhabitants *of* the country		その国の住民
1016	burn fossil *fuels*		化石燃料を燃やす
1017	the motive for the crime		犯罪の動機
1018	human instinct to fight		人間の闘争本能
1019	the legend of Robin Hood		ロビン・フッドの伝説
1020	the Roman Empire		ローマ帝国

単語	意味	書きこみ①	書きこみ②	書きこみ③	No.
ambition [æmbíʃən]	熱望				991
forecast [fɔ́ːrkæst]	予報				992
psychology [saikálədʒi]	心理学				993
labor [léibər]	労働				994
committee [kəmíti:]	委員会				995
physician [fizíʃən]	医者				996
philosophy [filásəfi]	哲学				997
affection [əfékʃən]	愛情				998
candidate [kǽndideit]	候補				999
bomb [bám]	爆弾				1000
priority [praió(:)rəti]	優先				1001
obstacle [ábstəkl]	障害				1002
appetite [ǽpitait]	食欲				1003
tension [ténʃən]	緊張				1004
tribe [tráib]	部族				1005
budget [bʌ́dʒit]	予算				1006
campaign [kæmpéin]	運動				1007
sorrow [sárou]	悲しみ				1008
satellite [sǽtəlait]	衛星				1009
insight [insait]	洞察				1010
cough [kɔ́(:)f]	せき				1011
fate [féit]	運命				1012
scheme [skíːm]	計画				1013
insult [insʌlt] 動 [insʌ́lt]	侮辱				1014
inhabitant [inhǽbitənt]	住民				1015
fossil [fá(:)səl]	化石				1016
motive [móutiv]	動機				1017
instinct [instiŋkt]	本能				1018
legend [lédʒənd]	伝説				1019
empire [émpaiər]	帝国				1020

No.	英語フレーズ	フレーズ書きこみ	日本語フレーズ
1021	live in the suburbs of London		ロンドンの郊外に住む
1022	study modern architecture		近代建築を学ぶ
1023	love and passion		愛と情熱
1024	the treatment of cancer		がんの治療
1025	persuade him with logic		彼を論理で説得する
1026	two dozen eggs		2ダースの卵
1027	a good harvest of rice		米の豊かな収穫
1028	the ingredients of the cake		ケーキの材料
1029	*test* the hypothesis		仮説を検証する
1030	the first voyage of Columbus		コロンブスの最初の航海
1031	the editor of a fashion magazine		ファッション雑誌の編集長
1032	have no option		選択の自由がない
1033	the southern hemisphere		南半球
1034	the mechanism of a clock		時計の仕組み
1035	Anthropologists study people.		人類学者は人間を研究する
1036	Greek tragedy		ギリシャ悲劇
1037	rcsistancc to antibiotics		抗生物質に対する耐性
1038	pay the bus fare		バスの運賃を払う
1039	pay the debt		借金を返す
1040	the high school curriculum		高校の教育課程
1041	the components of the body		人体の構成要素
1042	plant wheat and corn		小麦とコーンを植える
1043	modern English usage		現代英語の語法
1044	a sand castle		砂の城
1045	a terrible famine in Africa		アフリカのひどい飢饉
1046	animals in danger of extinction		絶滅の危機にある動物たち
1047	take money out of the purse		財布からお金を取り出す
1048	English folk music		イギリスの民族音楽
1049	the population explosion		人口爆発
1050	*a* large portion *of* your salary		給料の大部分

単語	意味	書きこみ①	書きこみ②	書きこみ③	No.
suburb [sʌ́bəːrb]	郊外				1021
architecture [ɑ́ːrkitektʃər]	建築				1022
passion [pǽʃən]	情熱				1023
cancer [kǽnsər]	がん				1024
logic [lɑ́dʒik]	論理				1025
dozen [dʌ́zn]	ダース				1026
harvest [hɑ́ːrvist]	収穫				1027
ingredient [ingríːdiənt]	材料				1028
hypothesis [haipɑ́θəsis]	仮説				1029
voyage [vɔ́iidʒ]	航海				1030
editor [éditər]	編集長				1031
option [ɑ́pʃən]	選択の自由				1032
hemisphere [hémisfiər]	半球				1033
mechanism [mékənizm]	仕組み				1034
anthropologist [ænθrəpɑ́lədʒist]	人類学者				1035
tragedy [trǽdʒədi]	悲劇				1036
antibiotic [æntibaiɑ́tik]	抗生物質				1037
fare [féər]	運賃				1038
debt [dét]	借金				1039
curriculum [kəríkjələm]	教育課程				1040
component [kəmpóunənt]	構成要素				1041
wheat [hwíːt]	小麦				1042
usage [júːsidʒ]	語法				1043
castle [kǽsl]	城				1044
famine [fǽmin]	飢饉				1045
extinction [ikstíŋkʃən]	絶滅				1046
purse [pə́ːrs]	財布				1047
folk [fóuk]	民族				1048
explosion [iksplóuʒən]	爆発				1049
portion [pɔ́ːrʃən]	部分				1050

2

Essential

No.	英語フレーズ	フレーズ書きこみ	日本語フレーズ
1051	marine organisms		海洋生物
1052	The Merchant of Venice		ヴェニスの商人
1053	ancient Greek myths		古代ギリシャの神話
1054	the small incidents of everyday life		日常生活の小さな出来事
1055	protect wildlife		野生生物を保護する
1056	the United States Congress		合衆国議会
1057	a boat in Tokyo Bay		東京湾に浮かぶ船
1058	the death penalty		死刑
1059	Japanese cultural heritage		日本の文化遺産
1060	American cultural diversity		アメリカの文化的多様性
1061	the thumb of my left hand		私の左手の親指
1062	history and geography		歴史と地理
1063	an important factor *in* success		成功の重要な要因
1064	discrimination *against* women		女性に対する差別
1065	the flu virus		インフルエンザウイルス
1066	the Statue of Liberty		自由の女神像
1067	a priest in the church		教会の神父
1068	a rock'n'roll pioneer		ロックンロールの先駆者
1069	personality traits		人格の特徴
1070	strong family bonds		家族の強いきずな
1071	go to the grocery store		食料品店に行く
1072	his secretary's desk		彼の秘書の机
1073	speak the local dialect		地元の方言を話す
1074	Galileo's astronomy		ガリレオの天文学
1075	today's youngsters		今日の子供たち
1076	a dangerous substance		危険な物質
1077	recent research findings		最近の研究による発見
1078	British military strategy		イギリスの軍事戦略
1079	his heart and lungs		彼の心臓と肺
1080	beat an opponent		敵を倒す

単語	意味	書きこみ①	書きこみ②	書きこみ③	No.
organism [ɔ́ːrgænizm]	生物				1051
merchant [mə́ːrtʃənt]	商人				1052
myth [míθ]	神話				1053
incident [ínsidənt]	出来事				1054
wildlife [wáildlaif]	野生生物				1055
congress [káŋgrəs]	議会				1056
bay [béi]	湾				1057
penalty [pénəlti]	刑				1058
heritage [héritidʒ]	遺産				1059
diversity [divə́ːrsəti]	多様性				1060
thumb [θʌ́m]	親指				1061
geography [dʒiágrəfi]	地理				1062
factor [fǽktər]	要因				1063
discrimination [diskriminéiʃən]	差別				1064
virus [váiərəs]	ウイルス				1065
statue [stǽtʃuː]	像				1066
priest [príːst]	神父				1067
pioneer [paiəníər]	先駆者				1068
trait [tréit]	特徴				1069
bond [bánd]	きずな				1070
grocery [gróusəri]	食料品				1071
secretary [sékrəteri]	秘書				1072
dialect [dáiəlekt]	方言				1073
astronomy [əstránəmi]	天文学				1074
youngster [jʌ́ŋstər]	子供				1075
substance [sʌ́bstəns]	物質				1076
finding [fáindiŋ]	発見				1077
strategy [strǽtədʒi]	戦略				1078
lung [lʌ́ŋ]	肺				1079
opponent [əpóunənt]	敵				1080

No.	英語フレーズ	フレーズ書きこみ	日本語フレーズ
1081	a religious ritual		宗教的な儀式
1082	the outcome of the race		レースの結果
1083	conservation groups		環境保護団体
1084	whales and other sea mammals		クジラなどの海の哺乳類
1085	NASA's space telescope		NASAの宇宙望遠鏡
1086	refugee camps in Palestine		パレスチナの難民キャンプ
1087	a strict dress code		厳しい服装規則
1088	the flavor of fresh fruit		新鮮なフルーツの風味
1089	the particles of light		光の粒子
1090	24-hour nursing		24時間看護
1091	commit suicide		自殺をする
1092	the natural habitat of bears		クマの自然生息地
1093	bullying in schools		学校のいじめ
1094	Dinosaurs died out.		恐竜は絶滅した
1095	the New York City Council		ニューヨーク市議会
1096	age and gender		年齢と性別
1097	have open heart surgery		心臓切開手術を受ける
1098	technological innovation		技術革新
1099	high-protein food		高タンパク質の食べ物
1100	enough sleep and nutrition		十分な睡眠と栄養
1101	prepare for *natural* disaster		自然災害に備える
1102	greenhouse gas emissions		温室効果ガスの排出
1103	monkeys and apes		猿と類人猿
1104	a single DNA molecule		1つのDNA分子
1105	the smell of sweat		汗の臭い
1106	a heart transplant operation		心臓移植の手術
1107	many species of birds		多くの種の鳥
1108	the tip of my finger		私の指の先
1109	raise sheep and cattle		羊と牛を育てる
1110	high population density		高い人口密度

単語	意味	書きこみ①	書きこみ②	書きこみ③	No.
ritual [rítʃuəl]	儀式				1081
outcome [áutkʌm]	結果				1082
conservation [kɑnsərvéiʃən]	環境保護				1083
mammal [mǽməl]	哺乳類				1084
telescope [téləskoup]	望遠鏡				1085
refugee [refjudʒíː]	難民				1086
code [kóud]	規則				1087
flavor [fléivər]	風味				1088
particle [pɑ́ːrtikl]	粒子				1089
nursing [nɔ́ːrsiŋ]	看護				1090
suicide [súːəsaid]	自殺				1091
habitat [hǽbitæt]	生息地				1092
bullying [búliiŋ]	いじめ				1093
dinosaur [dáinəsɔːr]	恐竜				1094
council [káunsl]	議会				1095
gender [dʒéndər]	性別				1096
surgery [sɔ́ːrdʒəri]	手術				1097
innovation [inəvéiʃən]	革新				1098
protein [próutiːn]	タンパク質				1099
nutrition [njuːtríʃən]	栄養				1100
disaster [dizǽstər]	災害				1101
emission [imíʃən]	排出				1102
ape [éip]	類人猿				1103
molecule [mɑ́ləkjuːl]	分子				1104
sweat [swét]	汗				1105
transplant [trǽnsplænt] 動 [— ́]	移植				1106
species [spíːʃiːz]	種				1107
tip [típ]	先				1108
cattle [kǽtl]	牛				1109
density [dénsəti]	密度				1110

2

Essential

No.	英語フレーズ	フレーズ書きこみ	日本語フレーズ
1111	the concept *of* time		時間の概念
1112	You look pale.		君は青白い顔をしている
1113	precious jewels		貴重な宝石
1114	a worker loyal *to* the company		会社に忠実な労働者
1115	be isolated *from* the world		世界から孤立している
1116	a generous offer		気前のよい申し出
1117	tropical rain forests		熱帯雨林
1118	*be* reluctant *to* talk about the past		過去について話したがらない
1119	a vague feeling of uneasiness		漠然とした不安感
1120	the vast land of Russia		ロシアの広大な土地
1121	numerous species of birds		たくさんの種の鳥
1122	move to a small rural town		小さな田舎の町に引っ越す
1123	the widespread use of cell phones		広まっている携帯電話の利用
1124	a complicated problem		複雑な問題
1125	make visible progress		目に見える進歩をとげる
1126	eat raw meat		生の肉を食べる
1127	live in a remote village		へんぴな村に住む
1128	need urgent action		緊急の行動を必要とする
1129	tell silly jokes		ばかな冗談を言う
1130	a striking contrast		いちじるしい対照
1131	provide adequate food		十分な食料を供給する
1132	a man of extraordinary talent		並はずれた才能の持ち主
1133	the odd couple		おかしな2人
1134	an abstract concept		抽象的な概念
1135	mutual understanding		相互の理解
1136	excessive use of alcohol		過度のアルコール摂取
1137	I'*m* ashamed *of* myself.		自分が恥ずかしい
1138	a tremendous amount of energy		とてつもない量のエネルギー
1139	Change is inevitable.		変化は避けられない
1140	pure gold		純金

単語	意味	書きこみ①	書きこみ②	書きこみ③	No.
concept [kánsept]	概念				1111
pale [péil]	青白い				1112
precious [préʃəs]	貴重な				1113
loyal [lɔ́iəl]	忠実な				1114
isolated [áisəleitid]	孤立している				1115
generous [dʒénərəs]	気前のよい				1116
tropical [trɑ́pikəl]	熱帯の				1117
reluctant [rilʌ́ktənt]	したがらない				1118
vague [véig]	漠然とした				1119
vast [vǽst]	広大な				1120
numerous [njú:mərəs]	たくさんの				1121
rural [rúərəl]	田舎の				1122
widespread [wáidspréd]	広まっている				1123
complicated [kɑ́mpləkeitəd]	複雑な				1124
visible [vízəbl]	目に見える				1125
raw [rɔ́:]	生の				1126
remote [rimóut]	へんぴな				1127
urgent [ɔ́:rdʒənt]	緊急の				1128
silly [síli]	ばかな				1129
striking [stráikiŋ]	いちじるしい				1130
adequate [ǽdikwət]	十分な				1131
extraordinary [ikstrɔ́:rdəneri]	並はずれた				1132
odd [ɑ́d]	おかしな				1133
abstract [ǽbstrækt]	抽象的な				1134
mutual [mjú:tʃuəl]	相互の				1135
excessive [iksésiv]	過度の				1136
ashamed [əʃéimd]	恥ずかしい				1137
tremendous [triméndəs]	とてつもない				1138
inevitable [inévitəbl]	避けられない				1139
pure [pjúər]	純粋な				1140

2
Essential

No.	英語フレーズ	フレーズ書きこみ	日本語フレーズ
1141	a stable condition		安定した状態
1142	be indifferent *to* politics		政治に無関心だ
1143	children's aggressive behavior		子供の攻撃的な行動
1144	the ultimate goal		究極の目標
1145	a quiet, shy girl		静かで内気な女の子
1146	solar energy		太陽エネルギー
1147	a profound meaning		深い意味
1148	a subtle difference		微妙な違い
1149	the Conservative Party		保守党
1150	a brave young soldier		勇敢な若い兵士
1151	feel intense pressure		強烈なプレッシャーを感じる
1152	alcoholic drinks like wine		ワインのようなアルコール飲料
1153	manual work		手を使う仕事 (肉体労働)
1154	cruel treatment of animals		動物に対する残酷な扱い
1155	rational thought		理性的な思考
1156	the initial stages of development		発達の最初の段階
1157	the body's immune *system*		人体の免疫機構
1158	the linguistic ability of children		子供の言語能力
1159	play a crucial role		重大な役割を果たす
1160	verbal communication		言葉によるコミュニケーション
1161	an optimistic view of the future		将来に関する楽観的な見方
1162	have flexible thinking		柔軟な考えを持っている
1163	I'm grateful *for* your help.		君の助けに感謝している
1164	a lively conversation		生き生きとした会話
1165	an overwhelming majority		圧倒的な多数
1166	an abundant supply of food		豊富な食料供給
1167	a selfish attitude		利己的な態度
1168	an ugly duckling		みにくいアヒルの子
1169	racial differences		人種の違い
1170	a prominent scientist		有名な科学者

⑺形容詞：本冊 p. 193 〜 197

単語	意味	書きこみ①	書きこみ②	書きこみ③	No.
stable [stéibl]	安定した				1141
indifferent [indífərənt]	無関心な				1142
aggressive [əɡrésiv]	攻撃的な				1143
ultimate [Áltimət]	究極の				1144
shy [ʃái]	内気な				1145
solar [sóulər]	太陽の				1146
profound [prəfáund]	深い				1147
subtle [sΛtl]	微妙な				1148
conservative [kənsə́ːrvətiv]	保守の				1149
brave [bréiv]	勇敢な				1150
intense [inténs]	強烈な				1151
alcoholic [ælkəhálik]	アルコールの				1152
manual [mǽnjuəl]	手を使う				1153
cruel [krúːəl]	残酷な				1154
rational [rǽʃənəl]	理性的な				1155
initial [iníʃəl]	最初の				1156
immune [imjúːn]	免疫の				1157
linguistic [liŋɡwístik]	言語の				1158
crucial [krúːʃəl]	重大な				1159
verbal [və́ːrbəl]	言葉による				1160
optimistic [ɑptimístik]	楽観的な				1161
flexible [fléksəbl]	柔軟な				1162
grateful [ɡréitfəl]	感謝している				1163
lively [láivli]	生き生きとした				1164
overwhelming [ouvərhwélmiŋ]	圧倒的な				1165
abundant [əbΛ́ndənt]	豊富な				1166
selfish [sélfiʃ]	利己的な				1167
ugly [Λɡli]	みにくい				1168
racial [réiʃəl]	人種の				1169
prominent [prámənənt]	有名な				1170

2

Essential

No.	英語フレーズ	フレーズ書きこみ	日本語フレーズ
1171	a controversial social *issue*		物議を呼ぶ社会問題
1172	the Federal Government		連邦政府
1173	a ridiculous error		ばかげたまちがい
1174	an imaginary country		架空の国
	an imaginative writer		想像力豊かな作家
	every trouble imaginable		想像しうるあらゆる困難
1175	the harsh realities of life		厳しい人生の現実
1176	a random choice		無作為な選択
1177	adolescent boys and girls		思春期の少年少女
1178	up-to-date fashions		最新の流行
1179	liberal politics		自由主義の政治
1180	the period prior *to* the war		戦争より前の時代
1181	do moderate exercise		適度な運動をする
1182	be fluent *in* English		英語が流ちょうだ
1183	an elaborate system		手の込んだシステム
1184	an incredible story		信じられない話
1185	radical changes		根本的な変化
1186	acid rain		酸性雨
1187	sign language for deaf people		耳が不自由な人のための手話
1188	a medieval castle		中世の城
1189	protect the ecological system		生態系を保護する
1190	without the slightest doubt		少しの疑いもなく
1191	be ignorant *of* the fact		その事実を知らない
1192	children's cognitive abilities		子供の認知能力
1193	It's absolutely necessary.		絶対に必要だ
1194	virtually every woman		ほとんどすべての女性
1195	somewhat better than last year		去年より多少よい
1196	It is merely bad luck.		単に運が悪いだけです

単語	意味	書きこみ①	書きこみ②	書きこみ③	No.
controversial [kɑntrəvə́ːrʃəl]	物議を呼ぶ				1171
federal [fédərəl]	連邦の				1172
ridiculous [ridíkjuləs]	ばかげた				1173
imaginary [imǽdʒəneri]	架空の				1174
imaginative [imǽdʒənətiv]	想像力豊かな				
imaginable [imǽdʒənəbl]	想像しうる				
harsh [hɑ́ːrʃ]	厳しい				1175
random [rǽndəm]	無作為な				1176
adolescent [ædəlésnt]	思春期の				1177
up-to-date [ʌ́ptədéit]	最新の				1178
liberal [líbərəl]	自由主義の				1179
prior [práiər]	前の				1180
moderate [mɑ́dərit]	適度な				1181
fluent [flúːənt]	流ちょうな				1182
elaborate [ilǽbərit]	手の込んだ				1183
incredible [inkrédəbl]	信じられない				1184
radical [rǽdikəl]	根本的な				1185
acid [ǽsid]	酸性の				1186
deaf [déf]	耳が不自由な				1187
medieval [miːdíːvəl]	中世の				1188
ecological [ekəlɑ́dʒikəl]	生態の				1189
slight [sláit]	少しの				1190
ignorant [ígnərənt]	知らない				1191
cognitive [kɑ́gnətiv]	認知の				1192
absolutely [ǽbsəluːtli]	絶対に				1193
virtually [və́ːrtʃuəli]	ほとんど				1194
somewhat [sʌ́mhwɑt]	多少				1195
merely [míərli]	単に				1196

2

Essential

No.	英語フレーズ	フレーズ書きこみ	日本語フレーズ
1197	There's literally nothing there.		そこには文字通り何もない
	the literal meaning of the word		その単語の文字通りの意味
	literary history		文学の歴史
	literate people in India		読み書きのできるインド人
1198	a seemingly impossible task		一見不可能な仕事
1199	regardless *of* age		年齢に関係なく
1200	thoroughly enjoy the party		パーティを徹底的に楽しむ

単語	意味	書きこみ①	書きこみ②	書きこみ③	No.
literally [lítərəli]	文字通りに				1197
literal [lítərəl]	文字通りの				
literary [lítərəri]	文学の				
literate [lítərət]	読み書きのできる				
seemingly [síːmiŋli]	一見				1198
regardless of A [rigáːrdləs]	Aに関係なく				1199
thoroughly [θɔ́ːrouli]	徹底的に				1200

2 Essential

Stage 3

Advanced Stage

"*All the world's a stage,*
And all the men and women merely players"
—— *Shakespeare*

* * *

この世はすべて1つの舞台，男も女も皆役者にすぎない。
—シェイクスピア

No.	英語フレーズ	フレーズ書きこみ	日本語フレーズ
1201	submit *to* authority		権威に服従する
1202	*be* tempted *to* call her		彼女に電話をかけたくなる
1203	The president will resign soon.		社長はまもなく辞任する
1204	conform *to* the rules		ルールに従う
1205	*be* confined *to* a small room		小さな部屋に閉じ込められる
1206	assemble small parts		小さい部品を組み立てる
1207	I *am* dedicated *to* my work.		私は仕事に身をささげている
1208	advocate peace		平和を主張する
1209	a thriving economy		繁栄する経済
1210	provoke a reaction		反応を引き起こす
1211	The market dictates prices.		市場が価格を決める
1212	exploit natural resources		天然資源を開発する
1213	surrender *to* the US army		アメリカ軍に降参する
1214	accurately reproduce the sound		正確に音を再生する
1215	acknowledge that a problem exists		問題があると認める
1216	swell like a balloon		風船のようにふくらむ
1217	Trees shed their leaves.		木々が葉を落とす
1218	the long and winding road		長く曲がりくねった道
1219	cite two examples		2つの例を引き合いに出す
1220	digest food		食べ物を消化する
1221	skip lunch		昼食を抜く
1222	*be* bound *by* tradition		伝統に縛られている
1223	dissolve sugar in water		水に砂糖を溶かす
1224	implement the secret plan		秘密の計画を実行する
1225	steer the ship		船を操縦する
1226	congratulate you *on* your success		君の成功を祝福する
1227	a designated smoking area		指定された喫煙場所
1228	violate the law		法律に違反する
1229	He is presumed innocent.		彼は無罪だと推定される
1230	recruit new staff		新しいスタッフを入れる

単語	意味	書きこみ①	書きこみ②	書きこみ③	No.
submit to A [səbmít]	Aに服従する				1201
tempt [témpt]	～を誘惑する				1202
resign [rizáin]	（～を）辞職する				1203
conform [kənfɔ́ːrm]	従う				1204
confine [kənfáin]	～を限定する				1205
assemble [əsémbl]	～を組み立てる				1206
dedicate A to B [dédikeit]	AをBにささげる				1207
advocate [ǽdvəkeit] 名 [ǽdvəkət]	～を主張する				1208
thrive [θráiv]	繁栄する				1209
provoke [prəvóuk]	～を引き起こす				1210
dictate [díkteit]	～を命じる				1211
exploit [iksplɔ́it]	～を利用する				1212
surrender [səréndər]	降伏する				1213
reproduce [riːprədjúːs]	～を再生する				1214
acknowledge [əknálidʒ]	～を認める				1215
swell [swél]	ふくらむ				1216
shed [ʃéd]	～を落とす				1217
wind [wáind]	曲がる				1218
cite [sáit]	～を引き合いに出す				1219
digest [daidʒést]	～を消化する				1220
skip [skíp]	～をとばす				1221
bind [báind]	～を縛る				1222
dissolve [dizálv]	（～を）溶解する				1223
implement [ímpləmənt]	～を実行する				1224
steer [stíər]	～を操縦する				1225
congratulate [kəngrǽtʃuleit]	～を祝福する				1226
designate [dézigneit]	～を指定する				1227
violate [váiəleit]	～を破る				1228
presume [prizjúːm]	～と推定する				1229
recruit [rikrúːt]	～を入れる				1230

3 Advanced

No.	英語フレーズ	フレーズ書きこみ	日本語フレーズ
1231	His birthday coincides *with* mine.		彼の誕生日は私のと重なる
1232	enforce the new law		新しい法律を施行する
1233	people displaced by war		戦争で国を追われた人々
1234	The shirts will shrink.		そのシャツは縮むだろう
1235	betray a good friend		親友を裏切る
1236	The group comprises ten members.		そのグループは10人から構成される
1237	indulge *in* bad habits		悪い習慣にふける
1238	penetrate deep into the jungle		ジャングルに奥深く入り込む
1239	a devastating effect on nature		自然に対する壊滅的な影響
1240	plunge *into* the water		水に突っ込む
1241	The ball bounces back.		ボールがはね返る
1242	contradict what he said		彼の言ったことと矛盾する
1243	prescribe medicine		薬を処方する
1244	oppress small nations		小国をしいたげる
1245	cherish a dream		夢を胸に抱く
1246	illuminate the road		道を照らす
1247	trigger war		戦争の引き金を引く
1248	commute from Chiba to Tokyo		千葉から東京に通勤する
1249	induce deep sleep		深い眠りを誘う
1250	utilize waste materials		廃棄物を利用する
1251	The stick snapped.		棒がポキンと折れた
1252	donate blood and organs		血液や臓器を提供する
1253	a newly hatched chick		かえったばかりのヒヨコ
1254	live in an enclosed space		閉ざされた空間で暮らす
1255	the prevailing view		広まっている考え方
1256	sigh deeply		深くため息をつく
1257	Oil leaked from the tank.		油がタンクから漏れた
1258	*be* compelled *to* work hard		重労働を強制される
1259	*be* crushed by the pressure		プレッシャーに押しつぶされる
1260	the ability *to* comprehend language		言語を理解する能力

⑴動詞：本冊 p. 211 〜 216

単語	意味	書きこみ①	書きこみ②	書きこみ③	No.
coincide [kouinsáid]	同時に起きる				1231
enforce [enfɔ́ːrs]	〜を施行する				1232
displace [displéis]	〜を故郷から追い出す				1233
shrink [ʃríŋk]	縮む				1234
betray [bitréi]	〜を裏切る				1235
comprise [kəmpráiz]	〜から構成される				1236
indulge in A [indʌ́ldʒ]	Aにふける				1237
penetrate [pénətreit]	（〜に）入り込む				1238
devastate [dévəsteit]	〜を壊滅させる				1239
A plunge into B [plʌ́ndʒ]	AがBに突っ込む				1240
bounce [báuns]	はねる				1241
contradict [kɑntrədíkt]	〜と矛盾する				1242
prescribe [priskráib]	〜を処方する				1243
oppress [əprés]	〜をしいたげる				1244
cherish [tʃériʃ]	〜を胸に抱く				1245
illuminate [ilúːmineit]	〜を照らす				1246
trigger [trígər]	〜のきっかけになる				1247
commute [kəmjúːt]	通勤する				1248
induce [indjúːs]	〜を誘う				1249
utilize [júːtəlaiz]	〜を利用する				1250
snap [snǽp]	ポキンと折れる				1251
donate [dóuneit]	〜を提供する				1252
hatch [hǽtʃ]	〜をかえす				1253
enclose [enklóuz]	〜を囲む				1254
prevail [privéil]	普及している				1255
sigh [sái]	ため息をつく				1256
leak [líːk]	漏れる				1257
compel [kəmpél]	〜に強制する				1258
crush [krʌ́ʃ]	〜を押しつぶす				1259
comprehend [kɑmprihénd]	〜を理解する				1260

3

Advanced

No.	英語フレーズ	フレーズ書きこみ	日本語フレーズ
1261	negotiate for peace		和平交渉をする
1262	persist throughout life		生涯を通じて残る
1263	multiply by five		5倍に増える
1264	conceive *of* life *as* a game		人生をゲームと考える
1265	compensate *for* the loss		損失を埋め合わせる
1266	suspend the project		計画を中止する
1267	stir emotions		感情をかきたてる
1268	soak a towel in hot water		湯にタオルを浸す
1269	refine techniques		技術に磨きをかける
1270	arouse her curiosity		彼女の好奇心をかきたてる
1271	Speech precedes writing.		話し言葉は書き言葉に先行する
1272	render water undrinkable		水を飲めなくする
1273	mount the engine in the car		車にエンジンをすえつける
1274	retreat to a safe distance		安全な距離まで退く
1275	startling results		驚くような結果
1276	No one dares *to* tell the truth.		真実を話す勇気がある人はいない
1277	a wide sphere of activity		幅広い活動範囲
1278	a sequence of events		一連の事件
1279	a large deposit in the bank		多額の銀行預金
1280	an opinion poll		世論調査
1281	proceed *with* caution		慎重に進む
1282	feel a great rage		激しい怒りを感じる
1283	a mathematical formula		数式
1284	the plot of the movie		その映画の筋
1285	beyond the scope of science		科学の範囲を越えて
1286	the socially accepted norm		社会的に認められた規範
1287	look at them in disgust		反感を持って彼らを見る
1288	make a small compromise		小さな妥協をする
1289	a production supervisor		生産監督者
1290	a strange paradox		奇妙な逆説

単語	意味	書きこみ①	書きこみ②	書きこみ③	No.
negotiate [nigóuʃieit]	交渉する				1261
persist [pərsíst]	持続する				1262
multiply [mʎltəplai]	～を増やす				1263
conceive [kənsíːv]	（～を）想像する				1264
compensate [kámpənseit]	埋め合わせる				1265
suspend [səspénd]	～を中止する				1266
stir [stə́ːr]	～をかきたてる				1267
soak [sóuk]	～を浸す				1268
refine [rifáin]	～を洗練する				1269
arouse [əráuz]	～を刺激する				1270
precede [prisíːd]	～に先行する				1271
render O C [réndər]	OをCに変える				1272
mount [máunt]	～をすえつける				1273
retreat [ritríːt]	退く				1274
startle [stáːrtl]	～を驚かせる				1275
dare (to) V [déər]	Vする勇気がある				1276
sphere [sfíər]	領域				1277
sequence [síːkwəns]	連続				1278
deposit [dipázit]	預金				1279
poll [póul]	世論調査				1280
caution [kɔ́ːʃən]	用心				1281
rage [réidʒ]	激怒				1282
formula [fɔ́ːrmjulə]	式				1283
plot [plát]	筋				1284
scope [skóup]	範囲				1285
norm [nɔ́ːrm]	規範				1286
disgust [disgʌ́st]	嫌悪				1287
compromise [kámprəmaiz]	妥協				1288
supervisor [súːpərvaizər]	監督者				1289
paradox [pǽrədaks]	逆説				1290

3

Advanced

No.	英語フレーズ	フレーズ書きこみ	日本語フレーズ
1291	nerve tissue		神経組織
1292	the breakdown of the family		家庭の崩壊
1293	a new peace initiative		新たな平和構想
1294	the social fabric of Japan		日本の社会組織
1295	newspaper publicity		新聞広告
1296	reach the summit		頂上に達する
1297	a flock of white sheep		白いヒツジの群れ
1298	prevent the spread of plague		疫病の広がりを防ぐ
1299	write a letter *in* haste		あわてて手紙を書く
1300	*take a* nap in the afternoon		午後にうたた寝をする
1301	America and its allies		アメリカとその同盟国
1302	the first draft of his novel		彼の小説の最初の草稿
1303	a dramatic spectacle		劇的な光景
1304	the major premise		大前提
1305	a valuable asset		価値ある財産
1306	suffer from *jet* lag		時差ぼけで苦しむ
1307	gene therapy		遺伝子療法
1308	receive a warm reception		あたたかいもてなしを受ける
1309	organic compounds		有機化合物
1310	the blessings of nature		自然の恵み
1311	the sensation of flying		飛んでいるような感覚
1312	the worst economic recession		最悪の不況
1313	the North Pole		北極
1314	a positive outlook *on* life		人生に対する肯定的な考え方
1315	every field of human endeavor		人間活動のあらゆる分野
1316	war without mercy		情け容赦のない戦争
1317	Chinese children work harder than *their* Japanese counterparts.		中国の子供は日本の子供よりよく勉強する
1318	a training session		訓練期間
1319	a wide spectrum of interests		広範囲の関心事
1320	avoid junk food		ジャンクフードを避ける

単語	意味	書きこみ①	書きこみ②	書きこみ③	No.
tissue [tíʃuː]	組織				1291
breakdown [bréikdaun]	崩壊				1292
initiative [iníʃiətiv]	構想				1293
fabric [fæbrik]	織物				1294
publicity [pʌblísəti]	宣伝				1295
summit [sʌ́mit]	頂上				1296
flock [flɑ́k]	群れ				1297
plague [pléig]	疫病				1298
haste [héist]	急ぐこと				1299
nap [nǽp]	うたた寝				1300
ally [ǽlai]	同盟国				1301
draft [drǽft]	下書き				1302
spectacle [spéktəkl]	光景				1303
premise [prémis]	前提				1304
asset [ǽset]	財産				1305
lag [lǽg]	遅れ				1306
therapy [θérəpi]	療法				1307
reception [risépʃən]	もてなし				1308
compound [kɑ́mpaund] 動 [kəmpáund]	化合物				1309
blessing [blésiŋ]	ありがたいもの				1310
sensation [senséiʃən]	感覚				1311
recession [riséʃən]	不景気				1312
pole [póul]	棒				1313
outlook [áutluk]	考え方				1314
endeavor [endévər]	活動				1315
mercy [mɚ́ːrsi]	慈悲				1316
A's counterpart [káuntərpɑːrt]	Aに相当するもの				1317
session [séʃən]	期間				1318
a spectrum of A [spéktrəm]	Aの変動範囲				1319
junk [dʒʌ́ŋk]	くず				1320

3
Advanced

No.	英語フレーズ	フレーズ書きこみ	日本語フレーズ
1321	the worship of God		神に対する崇拝
1322	*be* apt *to* forget names		名前を忘れやすい
1323	a humble attitude		謙虚な態度
1324	*be* entitled *to* the money		そのお金をもらう権利がある
1325	a valid reason for being late		遅れてくる正当な理由
1326	see a faint light		かすかな光が見える
1327	a stiff reply		堅苦しい答え
1328	for some obscure reason		はっきりとわからない理由で
1329	survive the fierce competition		激しい競争に生き残る
1330	the most acute problem		最も深刻な問題
1331	sit idle all day		何もせず一日座っている
1332	crude stone tools		粗末な石器
1333	be jealous *of* his success		彼の成功をねたむ
1334	his pregnant wife		彼の妊娠している妻
1335	*be* liable *to* forget it		それを忘れがちである
1336	a stubborn father		頑固な父親
1337	make a decent living		まともな暮らしをする
1338	a marvelous record		驚くべき記録
1339	a misleading expression		誤解を招く表現
1340	synthetic fiber		合成繊維
1341	classical music		クラシック音楽
1342	in the Muslim world		イスラム世界で
1343	anticipate the future		未来を予想する
1344	rub the skin with a towel		タオルで肌をこする
1345	dispose *of* garbage		ゴミを処分する
1346	refrain *from* smoking		タバコを吸うのを控える
1347	accumulate knowledge		知識を蓄積する
1348	boost the economy		経済を活気づける
1349	drag a heavy bag to the car		車まで重いかばんを引きずる
1350	revise the guidelines		ガイドラインを修正する

単語	意味	書きこみ①	書きこみ②	書きこみ③	No.
worship [wə́ːrʃip]	崇拝				1321
be apt to V [ǽpt]	Vしがちである				1322
humble [hʌ́mbl]	謙虚な				1323
be entitled to A [intáitld]	Aを得る権利がある				1324
valid [vǽlid]	妥当な				1325
faint [féint]	かすかな				1326
stiff [stíf]	堅い				1327
obscure [əbskjúər]	わかりにくい				1328
fierce [fíərs]	激しい				1329
acute [əkjúːt]	深刻な				1330
idle [áidl]	何もしていない				1331
crude [krúːd]	粗末な				1332
jealous [dʒéləs]	嫉妬深い				1333
pregnant [prégnənt]	妊娠している				1334
be liable to V [láiəbl]	Vしがちである				1335
stubborn [stʌ́bərn]	頑固な				1336
decent [díːsnt]	まともな				1337
marvelous [mɑ́ːrvələs]	驚くべき				1338
misleading [mislíːdiŋ]	誤解を招く				1339
synthetic [sinθétik]	合成の				1340
classical [klǽsikl]	クラシックの				1341
Muslim [mʌ́zləm]	イスラム教の				1342
anticipate [æntísəpeit]	～を予想する				1343
rub [rʌ́b]	～をこする				1344
dispose of A [dispóuz]	Aを処分する				1345
refrain [rifréin]	控える				1346
accumulate [əkjúːmjuleit]	～を蓄積する				1347
boost [búːst]	～を活気づける				1348
drag [drǽg]	～を引きずる				1349
revise [riváiz]	～を修正する				1350

3

Advanced

No.	英語フレーズ	フレーズ書きこみ	日本語フレーズ
1351	scratch your back		君の背中をかく
1352	roar like a lion		ライオンのようにほえる
1353	quote the Bible		聖書を引用する
1354	when roses bloom		バラの花が咲く頃
1355	insert the key into the hole		穴にかぎを差し込む
1356	patients awaiting a heart transplant		心臓移植を待つ患者
1357	dread going to the dentist		歯医者に行くのを恐れる
1358	conceal the fact *from* him		彼に事実を隠す
1359	Art enriches our lives.		芸術は人生を豊かにする
1360	cling *to* tradition		伝統に固執する
1361	surpass the US in technology		科学技術でアメリカにまさる
1362	suppress anger		怒りを抑える
1363	portray natural beauty		自然の美を描く
1364	the soaring price of oil		急上昇する石油の価格
1365	drain water *from* the tank		タンクから水を排出する
1366	glow in the dark		暗闇でボーッと光る
1367	migrate to California		カリフォルニアに移住する
1368	exclaim in surprise		驚いて叫ぶ
1369	exert a strong *influence*		強い影響を及ぼす
1370	disguise anger with a smile		笑顔で怒りを隠す
1371	accelerate the process of reform		改革の進行を加速する
1372	dwell in the forest		森の中に住む
1373	integrate immigrants *into* society		社会に移民を融けこませる
1374	weep all night long		一晩中泣く
1375	reassure the patient		患者を安心させる
1376	crawl into bed		ベッドまではって進む
1377	restrain inflation		インフレを抑制する
1378	resent being called foreigners		外国人と呼ばれるのに腹を立てる
1379	yell at the children		子供たちに大声で叫ぶ
1380	assess students' ability		学生の能力を評価する

⑷動詞：本冊 p. 233 〜 236

単語	意味	書きこみ①	書きこみ②	書きこみ③	No.
scratch [skrǽtʃ]	〜をかく				1351 ☐
roar [rɔ́ːr]	ほえる				1352 ☐
quote [kwóut]	〜を引用する				1353 ☐
bloom [blúːm]	咲く				1354 ☐
insert [insɔ́ːrt]	〜を差し込む				1355 ☐
await [əwéit]	〜を待つ				1356 ☐
dread [dréd]	〜を恐れる				1357 ☐
conceal [kənsíːl]	〜を隠す				1358 ☐
enrich [inrítʃ]	〜を豊かにする				1359 ☐
cling [klíŋ]	固執する				1360 ☐
surpass [sərpǽs]	〜にまさる				1361 ☐
suppress [səprés]	〜を抑える				1362 ☐
portray [pɔːrtréi]	〜を描く				1363 ☐
soar [sɔ́ːr]	急上昇する				1364 ☐
drain [dréin]	〜を排出する				1365 ☐
glow [glóu]	ボーッと光る				1366 ☐
migrate [máigreit]	移住する				1367 ☐
exclaim [ikskléim]	叫ぶ				1368 ☐
exert [igzɔ́ːrt]	〜を及ぼす				1369 ☐
disguise [disgáiz]	〜を隠す				1370 ☐
accelerate [ækséləreit]	〜を加速する				1371 ☐
dwell [dwél]	住む				1372 ☐
integrate [íntəgreit]	〜を融けこませる				1373 ☐
weep [wíːp]	泣く				1374 ☐
reassure [riːəʃúər]	〜を安心させる				1375 ☐
crawl [krɔ́ːl]	はって進む				1376 ☐
restrain [ristréin]	〜を抑制する				1377 ☐
resent [rizént]	〜に腹を立てる				1378 ☐
yell [jél]	大声で叫ぶ				1379 ☐
assess [əsés]	〜を評価する				1380 ☐

3

Advanced

No.	英語フレーズ	フレーズ書きこみ	日本語フレーズ
1381	carve her name in stone		石に彼女の名前を彫る
1382	halt global warming		地球温暖化を止める
1383	inspect the car *for* defects		欠陥がないか車を検査する
1384	tackle environmental problems		環境問題に取り組む
1385	omit the word		その言葉を省く
1386	chew food well		食べ物をよくかむ
1387	resume normal activities		ふだんの活動を再開する
1388	mold plastic products		プラスチック製品を作る
1389	*can* accommodate 800 people		800人を収容できる
1390	erase the data		データを消す
1391	can be inferred *from* the passage		文章から推量することができる
1392	revive the British economy		英国経済を生き返らせる
1393	contemplate marrying him		彼との結婚を考える
1394	The earth rotates once a day.		地球は日に1回回転する
1395	disrupt their lives		彼らの生活をかき乱す
1396	navigate by the stars		星によって進路を決める
1397	My whole body aches.		体中が痛む
1398	discard old ideas		古い考えを捨てる
1399	incorporate the Internet *into* the classroom		教室にインターネットを取り入れる
1400	overtake Japan in PC sales		パソコンの売上で日本を追い越す
1401	supplement your diet		食事を補う
1402	manipulate a computer		コンピュータを操作する
1403	nourish children's abilities		子供たちの能力を養う
1404	squeeze an orange		オレンジをしぼる
1405	depict him *as* a hero		英雄として彼を描く
1406	distract attention *from* the problem		問題から注意をそらす
1407	disclose his secret		彼の秘密を暴露する
1408	enroll *in* medical school		医学部に入学する
1409	nurture new technology		新しい科学技術を育てる
1410	speculate about the future		将来のことを推測する

単語	意味	書きこみ①	書きこみ②	書きこみ③	No.
carve [ká:rv]	〜を彫る				1381
halt [hɔ́:lt]	〜を止める				1382
inspect [inspékt]	〜を検査する				1383
tackle [tǽkl]	〜に取り組む				1384
omit [oumít]	〜を省く				1385
chew [tʃú:]	かむ				1386
resume [rizjú:m]	〜を再開する				1387
mold [móuld]	〜を作る				1388
accommodate [əkámədeit]	〜を収容できる				1389
erase [iréis]	〜を消す				1390
infer [infə́:r]	推量する				1391
revive [riváiv]	〜を生き返らせる				1392
contemplate [kántəmpleit]	〜を考える				1393
rotate [róuteit]	回転する				1394
disrupt [disrʌ́pt]	〜をかき乱す				1395
navigate [nǽvəgeit]	進路を決める				1396
ache [éik]	痛む				1397
discard [diská:rd]	〜を捨てる				1398
incorporate [inkɔ́:rpəreit]	〜を取り入れる				1399
overtake [ouvərtéik]	〜を追い越す				1400
supplement [sʌ́pləment]	〜を補う				1401
manipulate [mənípjuleit]	〜を操作する				1402
nourish [nɔ́:riʃ]	〜を養う				1403
squeeze [skwí:z]	〜をしぼる				1404
depict [dipíkt]	〜を描く				1405
distract [distrǽkt]	〜をそらす				1406
disclose [disklóuz]	〜を暴露する				1407
enroll [inróul]	入学する				1408
nurture [nɔ́:rtʃər]	〜を育てる				1409
speculate [spékjəleit]	推測する				1410

3

Advanced

No.	英語フレーズ	フレーズ書きこみ	日本語フレーズ
1411	prolong life		寿命を延ばす
1412	execute the murderer		殺人犯を処刑する
1413	uncover new evidence		新しい証拠を明らかにする
1414	tremble with fear		恐怖でふるえる
1415	seize the opportunity		チャンスをつかむ
1416	abolish slavery		奴隷制を廃止する
1417	scold my son _for_ being lazy		怠けたことで息子をしかる
1418	attain the goal		目標を達成する
1419	utter a word		言葉を発する
1420	flee _to_ free countries		自由な国に逃げる
1421	avoid offending others		他人を怒らせるのを避ける
1422	confess that I did it		私がやったと告白する
1423	postpone mak_ing_ a decision		決定するのを延期する
1424	drift like a cloud		雲のようにただよう
1425	weave cotton cloth		木綿の布を織る
1426	install solar panels on the roof		屋根にソーラーパネルを備えつける
1427	twist a wire		針金をねじ曲げる
1428	extract DNA _from_ blood		血液からDNAを取り出す
1429	bump _into_ someone		人にぶつかる
1430	Don't despise poor people.		貧しい人を軽蔑するな
1431	tolerate pain		苦痛を我慢する
1432	boast _of_ being rich		金持ちなのを自慢する
1433	The European economy is flourishing.		ヨーロッパ経済は栄えている
1434	disregard safety rules		安全規則を無視する
1435	Don't tease me!		私をからかうな
1436	reinforce the belief		信念を強める
1437	strive _to_ survive		生き残るために努力する
1438	coordinate movements with each other		互いに動きを合わせる
1439	yawn when you are bored		退屈なときにあくびをする
1440	hug and kiss him		彼を抱きしめキスする

単語	意味	書きこみ①	書きこみ②	書きこみ③	No.
prolong [prəlɔ́(ː)ŋ]	～を延ばす				1411
execute [éksəkjuːt]	～を処刑する				1412
uncover [ʌnkʌ́vər]	～を明らかにする				1413
tremble [trémbl]	ふるえる				1414
seize [síːz]	～をつかむ				1415
abolish [əbáliʃ]	～を廃止する				1416
scold [skóuld]	～をしかる				1417
attain [ətéin]	～を達成する				1418
utter [ʌ́tər]	～を発する				1419
flee [flíː]	逃げる				1420
offend [əfénd]	～を怒らせる				1421
confess [kənfés]	～と告白する				1422
postpone [poustpóun]	～を延期する				1423
drift [dríft]	ただよう				1424
weave [wíːv]	～を織る				1425
install [instɔ́ːl]	～を備えつける				1426
twist [twíst]	～をねじ曲げる				1427
extract [ikstrǽkt]	～を取り出す				1428
bump [bʌ́mp]	ぶつかる				1429
despise [dispáiz]	～を軽蔑する				1430
tolerate [táləreit]	～を我慢する				1431
boast [bóust]	自慢する				1432
flourish [flə́ːriʃ]	栄えている				1433
disregard [disrigáːrd]	～を無視する				1434
tease [tíːz]	～をからかう				1435
reinforce [riːinfɔ́ːrs]	～を強める				1436
strive [stráiv]	努力する				1437
coordinate [kouɔ́ːrdineit]	～を合わせる				1438
yawn [jɔ́ːn]	あくびをする				1439
hug [hʌ́g]	抱きしめる				1440

3 Advanced

No.	英語フレーズ	フレーズ書きこみ	日本語フレーズ
1441	combat global warming		地球温暖化と戦う
1442	knit a sweater		セーターを編む
1443	mental fatigue		精神疲労
1444	win fame and fortune		名声と富を得る
1445	The room is a mess.		部屋の中がめちゃくちゃだ
1446	death *with* dignity		尊厳死
1447	the Panama Canal		パナマ運河
1448	a long drought in Africa		アフリカの長い干ばつ
1449	give up in despair		絶望してあきらめる
1450	*at* intervals of ten minutes		10分の間隔で
1451	help him with his luggage		彼が荷物を持つのを手伝う
1452	*on* behalf *of* the class		クラスを代表して
1453	feel an impulse *to* shout		叫びたい衝動を感じる
1454	debris from an explosion		爆発による破片
1455	Beauty and the Beast		美女と野獣
1456	believe a foolish superstition		ばかげた迷信を信じる
1457	the illusion that Japan is safc		日本が安全だという幻想
1458	cotton thread		木綿の糸
1459	reduce salt intake		塩分の摂取量を減らす
1460	invite guests to the feast		宴会に客を招待する
1461	a seasonal transition		季節の移り変わり
1462	the misery of war		戦争の悲惨さ
1463	dangerous radiation		危険な放射線
1464	a log cabin		丸太小屋
1465	reach consensus *on* the issue		その問題で合意に達する
1466	do a *good* deed a day		1日に1つよい行いをする
1467	an old Chinese proverb		古い中国のことわざ
1468	Thank you for the compliment.		ほめ言葉をありがとう
1469	watch the candle flame		ろうそくの炎を見つめる
1470	*celebrate* their *wedding* anniversary		2人の結婚記念日を祝う

単語	意味	書きこみ①	書きこみ②	書きこみ③	No.
combat [kámbæt]	〜と戦う				1441
knit [nít]	〜を編む				1442
fatigue [fətíːg]	疲労				1443
fame [féim]	名声				1444
mess [més]	めちゃくちゃ				1445
dignity [dígniti]	尊厳				1446
canal [kənǽl]	運河				1447
drought [dráut]	干ばつ				1448
despair [dispéər]	絶望				1449
interval [íntərvəl]	間隔				1450
luggage [lʌ́gidʒ]	荷物				1451
behalf [bihǽf]	代表				1452
impulse [ímpʌls]	衝動				1453
debris [dəbríː]	破片				1454
beast [bíːst]	野獣				1455
superstition [suːpərstíʃən]	迷信				1456
illusion [ilʒúːʒən]	幻想				1457
thread [θréd]	糸				1458
intake [ínteik]	摂取量				1459
feast [fíːst]	宴会				1460
transition [trænzíʃən]	移り変わり				1461
misery [mízəri]	悲惨さ				1462
radiation [reidiéiʃən]	放射線				1463
log [lɔ́(ː)g]	丸太				1464
consensus [kənsénsəs]	合意				1465
deed [díːd]	行い				1466
proverb [právərb]	ことわざ				1467
compliment [kámplimənt]	ほめ言葉				1468
flame [fléim]	炎				1469
anniversary [ænəvə́ːrsəri]	記念日				1470

3

Advanced

No.	英語フレーズ	フレーズ書きこみ	日本語フレーズ
1471	Follow your conscience.		自分の良心に従え
1472	an expedition to the moon		月世界探検
1473	produce offspring		子孫をつくる
1474	my monthly allowance		僕の毎月のこづかい
1475	a newspaper headline		新聞の大見出し
1476	sign a peace treaty		平和条約に署名する
1477	a historical monument		歴史的な記念碑
1478	a worm in the apple		リンゴの中の虫
1479	a good remedy for colds		風邪のよい治療法
1480	a 20-volume encyclopedia		20巻の百科事典
1481	*catch a* glimpse *of* her face		彼女の顔がちらりと見える
1482	school personnel		学校の職員
1483	the triumph of science		科学の勝利
1484	reading, writing, and arithmetic		読み書き算数
1485	people with low self-esteem		自尊心の低い人々
1486	microbes in the soil		土壌にすむ微生物
1487	the odds *of* successful treatment		治療が成功する可能性
1488	a society in chaos		混沌とした社会
1489	control the destiny of mankind		人類の運命を支配する
1490	a disk five inches *in* diameter		直径5インチのディスク
1491	win the lottery		宝くじに当たる
1492	a souvenir shop in Hong Kong		香港のみやげ物屋
1493	walk along a mountain trail		山の小道を歩く
1494	a ratio of 10 to 1		10対1の比率
1495	fight with a sword		剣で戦う
1496	blow a whistle		笛を吹く
1497	public sentiment against slavery		奴隷制に対する国民感情 [世論]
1498	share *household* chores		家庭の雑用を分担する
1499	be treated with courtesy		礼儀正しい扱いを受ける
1500	the New York City mayor		ニューヨーク市長

単語	意味	書きこみ①	書きこみ②	書きこみ③	No.
conscience [kánʃəns]	良心				1471
expedition [ekspədíʃən]	探検				1472
offspring [ɔ́(ː)fspriŋ]	子孫				1473
allowance [əláuəns]	こづかい				1474
headline [hédlain]	大見出し				1475
treaty [tríːti]	条約				1476
monument [mánjumənt]	記念碑				1477
worm [wə́ːrm]	虫				1478
remedy [rémədi]	治療法				1479
encyclopedia [ensaikləpíːdiə]	百科事典				1480
glimpse [glímps]	ちらりと見えること				1481
personnel [pəːrsənél]	職員				1482
triumph [tráiəmf]	勝利				1483
arithmetic [əríθmətik] 形 [æriθmétik]	算数				1484
self-esteem [sélfistíːm]	自尊心				1485
microbe [máikroub]	微生物				1486
odds [ádz]	可能性				1487
chaos [kéiɑs]	混沌				1488
destiny [déstini]	運命				1489
diameter [daiǽmitər]	直径				1490
lottery [látəri]	宝くじ				1491
souvenir [suːvəníər]	みやげ物				1492
trail [tréil]	小道				1493
ratio [réiʃou]	比率				1494
sword [sɔ́ːrd]	剣				1495
whistle [hwísl]	笛				1496
sentiment [séntəmənt]	感情				1497
chore [tʃɔ́ːr]	雑用				1498
courtesy [kə́ːrtəsi]	礼儀正しさ				1499
mayor [méiər]	市長				1500

3

Advanced

No.	英語フレーズ	フレーズ書きこみ	日本語フレーズ
1501	video surveillance systems		映像監視システム
1502	a big black trash bag		大きな黒いゴミ袋
1503	gain wealth and prestige		富と名声を手に入れる
1504	police headquarters		警察本部
1505	explore the vast wilderness		広大な荒野を探検する
1506	the earth's orbit around the sun		太陽を回る地球の軌道
1507	have a personal bias against women		女性に対して個人的偏見を持つ
1508	the Republic of Ireland		アイルランド共和国
1509	This house is a bargain.		この家は掘り出し物だ
1510	in the domain of psychology		心理学の領域で
1511	a fragment of blue glass		青いガラスの破片
1512	the Andromeda Galaxy		アンドロメダ星雲
1513	sit on mother's lap		母親のひざの上に座る
1514	the deadline _for_ the report		レポートの締め切り
1515	faster than a bullet		弾丸よりも速く
1516	the safety of pedestrians		歩行者の安全
1517	a conversation full of wit		機知に富んだ会話
1518	a nuisance to others		他人の迷惑
1519	_meet_ the criteria _for_ safety		安全基準を満たす
1520	face economic hardship		経済的苦難に直面する
1521	the glory _of_ the British Empire		大英帝国の栄光
1522	walk along the pavement		歩道を歩く
1523	the British Navy		英国海軍
1524	a movie script		映画の台本
1525	the old-age pension		老齢年金
1526	the province of Quebec		ケベック州
1527	a surplus of food		食糧の余剰
1528	add moisture to the skin		肌に水分を加える
1529	a leather elbow patch		革のひじ当て
1530	_at_ an altitude of 30,000 feet		高度3万フィートで

単語	意味	書きこみ①	書きこみ②	書きこみ③	No.
surveillance [sərvéiləns]	監視				1501
trash [trǽʃ]	ゴミ				1502
prestige [prestíːʒ]	名声				1503
headquarters [hédkwɔːrtərz]	本部				1504
wilderness [wíldərnəs]	荒野				1505
orbit [ɔ́ːrbət]	軌道				1506
bias [báiəs]	偏見				1507
republic [ripʌ́blik]	共和国				1508
bargain [báːrgin]	掘り出し物				1509
domain [douméin]	領域				1510
fragment [frǽgmənt]	破片				1511
galaxy [gǽləksi]	星雲				1512
lap [lǽp]	ひざ				1513
deadline [dédlain]	締め切り				1514
bullet [búlit]	弾丸				1515
pedestrian [pədéstriən]	歩行者				1516
wit [wít]	機知				1517
nuisance [njúːsəns]	迷惑				1518
criteria [kraitíəriə]	基準				1519
hardship [háːrdʃip]	苦難				1520
glory [glɔ́ːri]	栄光				1521
pavement [péivmənt]	歩道				1522
navy [néivi]	海軍				1523
script [skrípt]	台本				1524
pension [pénʃən]	年金				1525
province [právins]	州				1526
surplus [sɔ́ːrpləs]	余剰				1527
moisture [mɔ́istʃər]	水分				1528
patch [pǽtʃ]	部分				1529
altitude [ǽltitjuːd]	高度				1530

3

Advanced

No.	英語フレーズ	フレーズ書きこみ	日本語フレーズ
1531	The thermometer shows 0℃.		温度計が0℃を示す
1532	pay college tuition		大学の授業料を支払う
1533	send Japanese troops abroad		日本の軍隊を海外に送る
1534	humans and other primates		人間と他の霊長類
1535	find flaws *in* his argument		彼の主張に欠陥を見つける
1536	his son and nephew		彼の息子と甥
1537	wear a silk garment		絹の衣服を身につける
1538	the diagnosis of disease		病気の診断
1539	industry and commerce		工業と商業
1540	the art of antiquity		古代の美術
1541	a small fraction *of* the money		その金のほんの一部
1542	the irony of fate		運命の皮肉
1543	have a nightmare		悪夢を見る
1544	a defect *in* the structure		構造上の欠陥
1545	a birth certificate		出生証明書
1546	prevent the decay of food		食品の腐敗を防ぐ
1547	prevent *soil* erosion		土壌の浸食を防ぐ
1548	a recipe for happiness		幸福の秘けつ
1549	the human skeleton		人間の骨格
1550	the grace of her movements		彼女のしぐさの優雅さ
1551	visit some Paris landmarks		パリの名所を訪ねる
1552	the symptoms of dementia		認知症の症状
1553	flesh and blood		肉と血
1554	collision *with* the earth		地球との衝突
1555	a hazard to health		健康にとって危険なもの
1556	the tomb of the unknown soldier		無名戦士の墓
1557	take daily injections		毎日注射を受ける
1558	a breakthrough *in* technology		技術の飛躍的進歩
1559	a leather bag		革のかばん
1560	a jewelry store		宝石店

単語	意味	書きこみ①	書きこみ②	書きこみ③	No.
thermometer [θərmάmətər]	温度計				1531
tuition [tjuːíʃən]	授業料				1532
troop [trúːp]	軍隊				1533
primate [práimeit]	霊長類				1534
flaw [flɔ́ː]	欠陥				1535
nephew [néfjuː]	甥				1536
garment [gάːrmənt]	衣服				1537
diagnosis [daiəgnóusis]	診断				1538
commerce [kάmərs]	商業				1539
antiquity [æntíkwəti]	古代				1540
fraction [frǽkʃən]	ほんの一部				1541
irony [áiərəni]	皮肉				1542
nightmare [náitmeər]	悪夢				1543
defect [díːfekt]	欠陥				1544
certificate [sərtífikət]	証明書				1545
decay [dikéi]	腐敗				1546
erosion [iróuʒən]	浸食				1547
recipe [résəpi]	秘けつ				1548
skeleton [skélitn]	骨格				1549
grace [gréis]	優雅さ				1550
landmark [lǽndmɑːrk]	名所				1551
dementia [diménʃə]	認知症				1552
flesh [fléʃ]	肉				1553
collision [kəlíʒən]	衝突				1554
hazard [hǽzərd]	危険なもの				1555
tomb [túːm]	墓				1556
injection [indʒékʃən]	注射				1557
breakthrough [bréikθruː]	飛躍的進歩				1558
leather [léðər]	革				1559
jewelry [dʒúːəlri]	宝石				1560

3 Advanced

No.	英語フレーズ	フレーズ書きこみ	日本語フレーズ
1561	read nonverbal cues		非言語的な合図を読み取る
1562	Call an ambulance right away.		すぐに救急車を呼べ
1563	a *real* estate agent		不動産業者
1564	an export commodity		輸出向けの商品
1565	check the departure time		出発時刻を確認する
1566	enter a new phase		新しい段階に入る
1567	a car thief		車泥棒
1568	Saint Valentine		聖バレンタイン
1569	painting and sculpture		絵と彫刻
1570	feel deep grief over his death		彼の死に深い悲しみを感じる
1571	drive in the fast lane		追い越し車線を走る
1572	predators like lions		ライオンのような捕食動物
1573	fluids like water and air		水や空気のような流体
1574	an incentive *to* work		仕事のはげみ
1575	the bride and her father		花嫁とその父
1576	military intervention *in* Iraq		イラクへの軍事介入
1577	win by a wide margin		大差で勝つ
1578	a biography of Einstein		アインシュタインの伝記
1579	marry without parental consent		親の同意なしに結婚する
1580	a smoking volcano		噴煙を上げる火山
1581	anti-government rebels		反政府の反逆者たち
1582	the metaphor of the "melting pot"		「人種のるつぼ」という比喩
1583	gun control legislation		銃規制の法律
1584	be struck by lightning		雷に打たれる
1585	the use of pesticides		殺虫剤の使用
1586	write a newspaper column		新聞のコラムを書く
1587	spread a rumor about a ghost		幽霊のうわさを広める
1588	tiny dust particles		細かいほこりの粒子
1589	a dialogue between two students		2人の学生の対話
1590	learn English in kindergarten		幼稚園で英語を学ぶ

単語	意味	書きこみ①	書きこみ②	書きこみ③	No.
cue [kjúː]	合図				1561
ambulance [ǽmbjələns]	救急車				1562
estate [istéit]	不動産				1563
commodity [kəmɑ́dəti]	商品				1564
departure [dipɑ́ːrtʃər]	出発				1565
phase [féiz]	段階				1566
thief [θíːf]	泥棒				1567
saint [séint]	聖者				1568
sculpture [skʌ́lptʃər]	彫刻				1569
grief [gríːf]	悲しみ				1570
lane [léin]	車線				1571
predator [prédətər]	捕食動物				1572
fluid [flúːid]	流体				1573
incentive [inséntiv]	はげみ				1574
bride [bráid]	花嫁				1575
intervention [intərvénʃən]	介入				1576
margin [mɑ́ːrdʒin]	差				1577
biography [baiɑ́grəfi]	伝記				1578
consent [kənsént]	同意				1579
volcano [vɑlkéinou]	火山				1580
rebel [rébl] 動 [ribél]	反逆者				1581
metaphor [métəfɔːr]	比喩				1582
legislation [ledʒisléiʃən]	法律				1583
lightning [láitniŋ]	雷				1584
pesticide [péstəsaid]	殺虫剤				1585
column [kɑ́ləm]	コラム				1586
rumor [rúːmər]	うわさ				1587
dust [dʌ́st]	ほこり				1588
dialogue [dáiəlɔ(ː)g]	対話				1589
kindergarten [kíndərgɑːrtn]	幼稚園				1590

3

Advanced

No.	英語フレーズ	フレーズ書きこみ	日本語フレーズ
1591	a patient with type 2 diabetes		2型糖尿病の患者
1592	the risk of obesity		肥満の危険
1593	get a patent for a new invention		新発明の特許を取る
1594	the first chapter of The Tale of Genji		源氏物語の第1章
1595	Buckingham Palace		バッキンガム宮殿
1596	do the laundry		洗濯をする
1597	patients in the ward		病棟の患者
1598	at the outbreak of the war		戦争がぼっ発したとき
1599	solve a difficult equation		難しい方程式を解く
1600	bones found by an archaeologist		考古学者に発見された骨
1601	political corruption		政治の腐敗
1602	germs and viruses		細菌とウイルス
1603	have revenue of $100,000		10万ドルの収入がある
1604	rely on your spouse		配偶者に頼る
1605	cholera epidemic		コレラの流行
1606	America's infant mortality rate		アメリカの幼児死亡率
1607	economy class syndrome		エコノミークラス症候群
1608	the retail price		小売りの値段
1609	take a large dose *of* vitamin C		大量のビタミンCを服用する
1610	alcoholic beverages		アルコール飲料
1611	regulate metabolism		新陳代謝を調整する
1612	a hybrid of two plants		2つの植物の交配種
1613	the sweet scent of roses		バラの甘い香り
1614	reduce inflammation in the eye		眼の炎症を軽減する
1615	take sleeping pills		睡眠薬を飲む
1616	be in grave danger		重大な危機にある
1617	fertile *soil*		肥えた土壌
1618	be hostile *to* the government		政府に反感を持つ
1619	Water is indispensable *to* life.		水は生命にとって不可欠だ
1620	an information-oriented society		情報志向の社会

単語	意味	書きこみ①	書きこみ②	書きこみ③	No.
diabetes [daiəbíːtəs]	糖尿病				1591
obesity [oubíːsəti]	肥満				1592
patent [pǽtnt]	特許				1593
chapter [tʃǽptər]	章				1594
palace [pǽləs]	宮殿				1595
laundry [lɔ́ːndri]	洗濯				1596
ward [wɔ́ːrd]	病棟				1597
outbreak [áutbreik]	ぼっ発				1598
equation [i(ː)kwéiʒən]	方程式				1599
archaeologist [ɑːrkiɑ́lədʒist]	考古学者				1600
corruption [kərʌ́pʃən]	腐敗				1601
germ [dʒə́ːrm]	細菌				1602
revenue [révənjuː]	収入				1603
spouse [spáus]	配偶者				1604
epidemic [epidémik]	流行				1605
mortality [mɔːrtǽləti]	死亡				1606
syndrome [síndroum]	症候群				1607
retail [ríːteil]	小売り				1608
dose [dóus]	量				1609
beverage [bévəridʒ]	飲料				1610
metabolism [mətǽbəlizm]	新陳代謝				1611
hybrid [háibrid]	交配種				1612
scent [sént]	香り				1613
inflammation [ìnfləméiʃən]	炎症				1614
pill [píl]	薬				1615
grave [gréiv]	重大な				1616
fertile [fɔ́ːrtəl]	肥えた				1617
hostile [hɑ́stəl]	反感を持つ				1618
indispensable [indispénsəbl]	不可欠な				1619
oriented [ɔ́ːrientid]	志向の				1620

3 Advanced

No.	英語フレーズ	フレーズ書きこみ	日本語フレーズ
1621 ☐	a splendid view		すばらしい景色
1622 ☐	a competent teacher		有能な教師
1623 ☐	supreme joy		最高の喜び
1624 ☐	straightforward language		わかりやすい言葉遣い
1625 ☐	a land sacred to Islam		イスラム教徒の聖地
1626 ☐	take bold action		大胆な行動をとる
1627 ☐	feel uneasy about the future		将来について不安な気持ちになる
1628 ☐	neat clothes		きちんとした服
1629 ☐	a shallow river		浅い川
1630 ☐	make a fake cake		にせ物のケーキを作る
1631 ☐	a superficial difference		表面的な違い
1632 ☐	a completely absurd idea		まったくばかげた考え
1633 ☐	fragile items		壊れやすい物
1634 ☐	a girl from a respectable family		ちゃんとした家の娘
☐	be respectful *to* elders		年上の人に敬意を表する
☐	schools in the respective areas		それぞれの地区の学校
1635 ☐	a magnificent view		すばらしい光景
1636 ☐	an infinite *number* of stars		無限の数の星
1637 ☐	a comprehensive study		包括的研究
1638 ☐	a steep slope		険しい坂
1639 ☐	the gross domestic product		国内総生産 (=GDP)
1640 ☐	prepare for subsequent events		次に起こる出来事に備える
1641 ☐	my sincere apologies		私の心からの謝罪
1642 ☐	a toxic gas		有毒なガス
1643 ☐	take a neutral position		中立の立場をとる
1644 ☐	a diligent student		勤勉な学生
1645 ☐	have a sore throat		のどが痛い
1646 ☐	drink contaminated water		汚染された水を飲む
1647 ☐	an ambiguous expression		あいまいな表現
1648 ☐	an oral examination		口述の試験

単語	意味	書きこみ①	書きこみ②	書きこみ③	No.
splendid [spléndid]	すばらしい				1621
competent [kámpətənt]	有能な				1622
supreme [sjuprí:m]	最高の				1623
straightforward [streitfɔ́:rwərd]	わかりやすい				1624
sacred [séikrid]	神聖な				1625
bold [bóuld]	大胆な				1626
uneasy [ʌní:zi]	不安な				1627
neat [ní:t]	きちんとした				1628
shallow [ʃǽlou]	浅い				1629
fake [féik]	にせ物の				1630
superficial [sju:pərfíʃəl]	表面的な				1631
absurd [əbsə́:rd]	ばかげた				1632
fragile [frǽdʒəl]	壊れやすい				1633
respectable [rispéktəbl]	ちゃんとした				1634
respectful [rispéktfl]	敬意を表する				
respective [rispéktiv]	それぞれの				
magnificent [mægnífisnt]	すばらしい				1635
infinite [ínfənət]	無限の				1636
comprehensive [kɑmprihénsiv]	包括的な				1637
steep [stí:p]	険しい				1638
gross [gróus]	総計の				1639
subsequent [sʌ́bsikwənt]	次に起こる				1640
sincere [sinsíər]	誠実な				1641
toxic [tɑ́ksik]	有毒な				1642
neutral [njú:trəl]	中立の				1643
diligent [dílidʒənt]	勤勉な				1644
sore [sɔ́:r]	痛い				1645
contaminated [kəntǽmineitid]	汚染された				1646
ambiguous [æmbígjuəs]	あいまいな				1647
oral [ɔ́:rəl]	口述の				1648

3

Advanced

No.	英語フレーズ	フレーズ書きこみ	日本語フレーズ
1649	spend a restless night		落ち着かない夜を過ごす
1650	smell like rotten eggs		腐った卵のようににおう
1651	vigorous activity		精力的な活動
1652	an immense amount of information		莫大な量の情報
1653	metropolitan areas		大都市圏
1654	be punctual for an appointment		約束の時間をきっちり守る
1655	a solitary old man		孤独な老人
1656	take collective action		集団行動を起こす
1657	break off diplomatic relations		外交関係を断絶する
1658	a nasty smell		不快なにおい
1659	a helpless baby		無力な赤ん坊
1660	give explicit instructions		明確な指示を与える
1661	His company *went* bankrupt.		彼の会社は破産した
1662	the hope of eternal life		永遠の命の望み
1663	the sole survivor		唯一の生存者
1664	sour grapes		すっぱいブドウ
1665	a notable exception		注目すべき例外
1666	an affluent society		裕福な社会
1667	a naked man		裸の男
1668	the vocal organ		発声器官
1669	feminine beauty		女性の美しさ
1670	sit down in a vacant seat		空いている席に座る
1671	native and exotic animals		在来と外来の動物
1672	rigid rules		厳格な規則
1673	humid summer weather		夏の蒸し暑い天気
1674	an outstanding scholar		傑出した学者
1675	*be* addicted *to* drugs		麻薬中毒である
1676	be vulnerable *to* attack		攻撃を受けやすい
1677	spontaneous laughter		自然に起こる笑い
1678	be greedy for money		金にどん欲だ

単語	意味	書きこみ①	書きこみ②	書きこみ③	No.
restless [réstləs]	落ち着かない				1649
rotten [rátn]	腐った				1650
vigorous [vígərəs]	精力的な				1651
immense [iméns]	莫大な				1652
metropolitan [metrəpálitən]	大都市の				1653
punctual [pʌ́ŋktʃuəl]	時間をきっちり守る				1654
solitary [sáliteri]	孤独な				1655
collective [kəléktiv]	集団の				1656
diplomatic [dipləmǽtik]	外交の				1657
nasty [nǽsti]	不快な				1658
helpless [hélplis]	無力な				1659
explicit [iksplísit]	明確な				1660
bankrupt [bǽŋkrʌpt]	破産した				1661
eternal [itə́ːrnəl]	永遠の				1662
sole [sóul]	唯一の				1663
sour [sáuər]	すっぱい				1664
notable [nóutəbl]	注目すべき				1665
affluent [ǽfluənt]	裕福な				1666
naked [néikid]	裸の				1667
vocal [vóukl]	声の				1668
feminine [féminin]	女性の				1669
vacant [véikənt]	空いている				1670
exotic [igzátik]	外来の				1671
rigid [rídʒid]	厳格な				1672
humid [hjúːmid]	蒸し暑い				1673
outstanding [autstǽndiŋ]	傑出した				1674
addicted [ədíktid]	中毒である				1675
vulnerable [vʌ́lnərəbl]	受けやすい				1676
spontaneous [spantéiniəs]	自然に起こる				1677
greedy [gríːdi]	どん欲な				1678

No.	英語フレーズ	フレーズ書きこみ	日本語フレーズ
1679	a trivial matter		ささいな事柄
1680	Japan's per capita income		日本の一人当たりの国民所得
1681	the risks inherent *in* the sport		そのスポーツに元から伴う危険
1682	a promising new actress		前途有望な新人女優
1683	physiological reactions		生理的な反応
1684	clinical *trials* of new drugs		新薬の臨床試験
1685	chronic disease		慢性の病気
1686	divisions of geological time		地質学的な時代区分
1687	countless species of insects		無数の種類の昆虫
1688	innate ability to learn		先天的な学習能力
1689	be alert *to* every sound		あらゆる音に用心する
1690	autonomous cars		自動運転車
1691	occur simultaneously		同時に起こる
1692	utterly different from others		他人とまったく異なる
1693	change drastically		劇的に変化する
1694	*not* necessarily true		必ずしも本当でない
1695	He always tells the truth, thereby avoiding trouble.		彼はいつも真実を述べ、そうすることで、面倒を避けている
1696	speak frankly		率直に話す
1697	the two cities, namely, Paris and Tokyo		その2つの都市、すなわちパリと東京
1698	He tried hard, hence his success.		彼は努力した。だから成功した。
1699	pay bills via the Internet		インターネット経由で代金を払う
1700	owing *to* lack of fuel		燃料不足のために

⑹形容詞, ⑺副詞・その他：本冊 p. 277 ～ 280

単語	意味	書きこみ①	書きこみ②	書きこみ③	No.
trivial [tríviəl]	ささいな				1679
per capita [pər kǽpətə]	一人当たりの				1680
inherent [inhíərənt]	元から伴う				1681
promising [prámisiŋ]	前途有望な				1682
physiological [fiziəládʒikl]	生理的な				1683
clinical [klínikl]	臨床の				1684
chronic [kránik]	慢性の				1685
geological [dʒiːəládʒikl]	地質学的な				1686
countless [káuntləs]	無数の				1687
innate [inéit]	先天的な				1688
alert [əlɔ́ːrt]	用心する				1689
autonomous [ɔːtánəməs]	自動の				1690
simultaneously [saiməltéiniəsli]	同時に				1691
utterly [ʌ́tərli]	まったく				1692
drastically [drǽstikəli]	劇的に				1693
necessarily [nesəsérəli]	必ずしも				1694
thereby [ðeərbái]	そうすることで				1695
frankly [víːə]	率直に				1696
namely [néimli]	すなわち				1697
hence [frǽŋkli]	だから				1698
via A [héns]	前 A経由で				1699
owing to A [óuiŋ]	前 Aのために				1700

3
Advanced

129

Stage 4

Final Stage

*"Live as if you were to die tomorrow.
Learn as if you were to live forever."*

—— *Gandhi*

* * *

明日死ぬかのように生きよ。
　永遠に生きるかのように学べ。—ガンジー

No.	英語フレーズ	フレーズ書きこみ	日本語フレーズ
1701 ☐	clarify the meaning of the word		単語の意味を明らかにする
1702 ☐	smash a bottle		ビンを粉々に砕く
1703 ☐	mourn Gandhi's death		ガンジーの死を悲しむ
1704 ☐	summon the police		警察を呼ぶ
1705 ☐	shatter windows		窓を粉々にする
1706 ☐	linger in my memory		私の記憶に残る
1707 ☐	lament the shortness of life		人生の短さを嘆く
1708 ☐	*be* endowed *with* a talent		才能に恵まれる
1709 ☐	rejoice in the success		成功を喜ぶ
1710 ☐	allocate resources		資源を配分する
1711 ☐	slap his face		彼の顔をピシャリと打つ
1712 ☐	contend *that* money cannot buy happiness		お金で幸福は買えないと主張する
1713 ☐	swear never to drink again		二度と酒を飲まないと誓う
1714 ☐	can discern the difference		違いを識別することができる
1715 ☐	degrade the environment		環境を悪化させる
1716 ☐	erect barriers		障壁を築く
1717 ☐	testify in court		法廷で証言する
1718 ☐	spur him into action		行動へと彼を駆りたてる
1719 ☐	roam the streets freely		自由に街を歩き回る
1720 ☐	frown *on* smoking		喫煙にまゆをひそめる
1721 ☐	lure tourists to Japan		日本に観光客を呼び込む
1722 ☐	defy gravity		重力に逆らう
1723 ☐	stroll in the park		公園をぶらつく
1724 ☐	rattle the windows		窓をがたがた鳴らす
1725 ☐	reconcile religion *with* science		宗教と科学を調和させる
1726 ☐	blur the distinction		区別をぼやかす
1727 ☐	soothe a crying child		泣く子供をなだめる
1728 ☐	impair learning ability		学習能力を低下させる
1729 ☐	comply *with* the standards		基準に従う
1730 ☐	pierce my ears		耳に穴をあける

単語	意味	書きこみ①	書きこみ②	書きこみ③	No.
clarify [klǽrifai]	〜を明らかにする				1701
smash [smǽʃ]	〜を粉々に砕く				1702
mourn [mɔ́ːrn]	〜を悲しむ				1703
summon [sʌ́mən]	〜を呼ぶ				1704
shatter [ʃǽtər]	〜を粉々にする				1705
linger [líŋgər]	残る				1706
lament [ləmént]	〜を嘆く				1707
endow [indáu]	〜に恵まれる				1708
rejoice [ridʒɔ́is]	喜ぶ				1709
allocate [ǽləkeit]	〜を配分する				1710
slap [slǽp]	〜をピシャリと打つ				1711
contend [kənténd]	〜と主張する				1712
swear [swéər]	〜と誓う				1713
discern [disɔ́ːrn]	〜を識別する				1714
degrade [digréid]	〜を悪化させる				1715
erect [irékt]	〜を築く				1716
testify [téstəfai]	証言する				1717
spur [spɔ́ːr]	〜を駆りたてる				1718
roam [róum]	〜を歩き回る				1719
frown [fráun]	まゆをひそめる				1720
lure [ljúər]	〜を呼び込む				1721
defy [difái]	〜に逆らう				1722
stroll [stróul]	ぶらつく				1723
rattle [rǽtl]	〜をがたがた鳴らす				1724
reconcile [rékənsail]	〜を調和させる				1725
blur [blɔ́ːr]	〜をぼやかす				1726
soothe [súːð]	〜をなだめる				1727
impair [impéər]	〜を低下させる				1728
comply [kəmplái]	従う				1729
pierce [píərs]	〜に穴をあける				1730

No.	英語フレーズ	フレーズ書きこみ	日本語フレーズ
1731	stumble on the stairs		階段でつまずく
1732	hinder economic development		経済の発展をさまたげる
1733	mock her efforts		彼女の努力をあざける
1734	embody the spirit of the age		時代の精神を具現する
1735	stalk the prey		獲物に忍び寄る
1736	proclaim that Japan is safe		日本は安全だと宣言する
1737	The audience applauds.		観客が拍手する
1738	inflict pain _on_ other people		人に苦痛を与える
1739	merge _with_ the company		その会社と合併する
1740	People were evacuated from the area.		人々はその地域から避難した
1741	What is done cannot be undone.		一度したことは元に戻らない
1742	poke him in the ribs		彼のわき腹を突く
1743	be haunted by memories of war		戦争の記憶につきまとわれる
1744	adhere _to_ the international standards		国際基準を固く守る
1745	compile a list of customers		顧客のリストをまとめる
1746	The flowers will wither in the cold.		花は寒さでしぼむだろう
1747	stun the audience		聴衆をびっくりさせる
1748	choke on a piece of food		食べ物でのどがつまる
1749	His health will deteriorate.		彼の健康状態は悪化するだろう
1750	dump garbage in the street		通りにゴミを捨てる
1751	murmur in a low voice		低い声でつぶやく
1752	delete old emails		古いeメールを削除する
1753	inhibit the growth of bacteria		バクテリアの成長を阻害する
1754	divert attention _from_ the fact		事実から注意をそらす
1755	tame wild animals		野生動物を飼いならす
1756	reap large rewards		大きな報酬を手に入れる
1757	affirm that it is true		それは本当だと断言する
1758	be immersed _in_ a different culture		異なる文化に浸る
1759	My license expires next month.		私の免許は来月に期限が切れる
1760	embark _on_ a new adventure		新しい冒険に乗り出す

単語	意味	書きこみ①	書きこみ②	書きこみ③	No.
stumble [stʌ́mbl]	つまずく				1731
hinder [híndər]	〜をさまたげる				1732
mock [mák]	〜をあざける				1733
embody [imbádi]	〜を具現する				1734
stalk [stɔ́ːk]	〜に忍び寄る				1735
proclaim [prəkléim]	〜と宣言する				1736
applaud [əplɔ́ːd]	拍手する				1737
inflict [inflíkt]	〜を与える				1738
merge [mɔ́ːrdʒ]	合併する				1739
evacuate [ivǽkjueit]	〜を避難させる				1740
undo [ʌndúː]	〜を元に戻す				1741
poke [póuk]	〜を突く				1742
haunt [hɔ́ːnt]	〜につきまとう				1743
adhere [ədhíər]	固く守る				1744
compile [kəmpáil]	〜をまとめる				1745
wither [wíðər]	しぼむ				1746
stun [stʌ́n]	〜をびっくりさせる				1747
choke [tʃóuk]	のどがつまる				1748
deteriorate [ditíəriəreit]	悪化する				1749
dump [dʌ́mp]	〜を捨てる				1750
murmur [mɔ́ːrmər]	つぶやく				1751
delete [dilíːt]	〜を削除する				1752
inhibit [inhíbət]	〜を阻害する				1753
divert [divɔ́ːrt]	〜をそらす				1754
tame [téim]	〜を飼いならす				1755
reap [ríːp]	〜を手に入れる				1756
affirm [əfɔ́ːrm]	〜と断言する				1757
immerse [imɔ́ːrs]	浸る				1758
expire [ikspáiər]	期限が切れる				1759
embark [embáːrk]	乗り出す				1760

4
Final

No.	英語フレーズ	フレーズ書きこみ	日本語フレーズ
1761	vow to fight		戦うことを誓う
1762	foresee the future		未来を予知する
1763	adore him as a god		神として彼を崇拝する
1764	yearn *for* freedom		自由を切望する
1765	undermine the US position		アメリカの立場を弱める
1766	suck blood from humans		人間の血を吸う
1767	pledge to support them		彼らを支持することを誓う
1768	intrude *on* his privacy		彼のプライバシーに立ち入る
1769	sue a doctor		医者を訴える
1770	distort the facts		事実を歪曲する
1771	extinguish the fire		火を消す
1772	preach to the crowd		群衆に説教する
1773	curb population growth		人口増加を抑制する
1774	withstand high temperatures		高温に耐える
1775	dip the meat in the sauce		ソースに肉をひたす
1776	recite poetry		詩を暗唱する
1777	thrust the money into his pocket		彼のポケットにお金を押し込む
1778	plead *with* her to come back		彼女に戻るよう嘆願する
1779	humiliate him in front of others		人前で彼に恥をかかせる
1780	discharge waste into rivers		川に廃水を放出する
1781	condemn his behavior		彼の振る舞いを非難する
1782	retrieve information		情報を検索する
1783	shrug your shoulders		肩をすくめる
1784	evoke a response		反応を呼び起こす
1785	fetch water from the river		川から水を取ってくる
1786	flatter the boss		上司におせじを言う
1787	write prose and poetry		散文と詩を書く
1788	the textile industry		織物工業
1789	cut timber		材木を切る
1790	masterpieces of French art		フランス美術の傑作

単語	意味	書きこみ①	書きこみ②	書きこみ③	No.
vow [váu]	～を誓う				1761
foresee [fɔːrsíː]	～を予知する				1762
adore [ədɔ́ːr]	～を崇拝する				1763
yearn [jə́ːrn]	切望する				1764
undermine [ʌndərmáin]	～を弱める				1765
suck [sʌ́k]	～を吸う				1766
pledge [plédʒ]	～を誓う				1767
intrude [intrúːd]	立ち入る				1768
sue [sjúː]	～を訴える				1769
distort [distɔ́ːrt]	～を歪曲する				1770
extinguish [ikstíŋgwiʃ]	～を消す				1771
preach [príːtʃ]	説教する				1772
curb [kə́ːrb]	～を抑制する				1773
withstand [wiðstǽnd]	～に耐える				1774
dip [díp]	～をひたす				1775
recite [risáit]	～を暗唱する				1776
thrust [θrʌ́st]	～を押し込む				1777
plead [plíːd]	嘆願する				1778
humiliate [hjuːmílieit]	～に恥をかかせる				1779
discharge [distʃáːrdʒ]	～を放出する				1780
condemn [kəndém]	～を非難する				1781
retrieve [ritríːv]	～を検索する				1782
shrug [ʃrʌ́g]	～をすくめる				1783
evoke [ivóuk]	～を呼び起こす				1784
fetch [fétʃ]	～を取ってくる				1785
flatter [flǽtər]	～におせじを言う				1786
prose [próuz]	散文				1787
textile [tékstail]	織物				1788
timber [tímbər]	材木				1789
masterpiece [mǽstərpiːs]	傑作				1790

4 Final

No.	英語フレーズ	フレーズ書きこみ	日本語フレーズ
1791 ☐	an anti-government riot		反政府の暴動
1792 ☐	a train carriage		列車の車両
1793 ☐	breathing apparatus		呼吸装置
1794 ☐	*make a* fuss *about* nothing		くだらないことに大騒ぎする
1795 ☐	a vitamin deficiency		ビタミンの欠乏
1796 ☐	the heir *to* a fortune		財産の相続人
1797 ☐	a jungle *at* the equator		赤道直下のジャングル
1798 ☐	import petroleum		石油を輸入する
1799 ☐	an evil witch		邪悪な魔女
1800 ☐	Water changes into vapor.		水が蒸気に変わる
1801 ☐	a space probe		宇宙探査機
1802 ☐	expertise *in* programming		プログラミングの専門知識
1803 ☐	a look of scorn		軽蔑のまなざし
1804 ☐	the prophets of the Bible		聖書の預言者
1805 ☐	a cool breeze from the sea		海からの涼しいそよ風
1806 ☐	punishment for sin		罪に対する罰
1807 ☐	a surge in blood sugar		血糖の急増
1808 ☐	a complement to medical treatment		医療を補うもの
1809 ☐	wait in a queue		一列で待つ
1810 ☐	a high-stakes poker game		賭け金の高いポーカー
1811 ☐	the French ambassador *to* Japan		駐日フランス大使
1812 ☐	the judge and jury		裁判官と陪審員 (団)
1813 ☐	a cluster *of* neurons		ニューロンの集団
1814 ☐	a lump on the head		頭のこぶ
1815 ☐	the green meadow		緑の牧草地
1816 ☐	accomplish a remarkable feat		すばらしい偉業をなしとげる
1817 ☐	artistic temperament		芸術的な気質
1818 ☐	feel a chill		寒気を感じる
1819 ☐	electrical appliances		電気器具
1820 ☐	his predecessor as manager		彼の前任の経営者

単語	意味	書きこみ①	書きこみ②	書きこみ③	No.
riot [ráiət]	暴動				1791
carriage [kǽridʒ]	車両				1792
apparatus [æpərǽtəs]	装置				1793
fuss [fʌ́s]	大騒ぎ				1794
deficiency [difíʃənsi]	欠乏				1795
heir [éər]	相続人				1796
equator [ikwéitər]	赤道				1797
petroleum [pitróuliəm]	石油				1798
witch [wítʃ]	魔女				1799
vapor [véipər]	蒸気				1800
probe [próub]	探査機				1801
expertise [ekspəːrtíːz]	専門知識				1802
scorn [skɔ́ːrn]	軽蔑				1803
prophet [práfit]	預言者				1804
breeze [bríːz]	そよ風				1805
sin [sín]	罪				1806
surge [sə́ːrdʒ]	急増				1807
complement [kámpləmənt]	補うもの				1808
queue [kjúː]	列				1809
stake [stéik]	賭け金				1810
ambassador [æmbǽsədər]	大使				1811
jury [dʒúəri]	陪審員				1812
cluster [klʌ́stər]	集団				1813
lump [lʌ́mp]	こぶ				1814
meadow [médou]	牧草地				1815
feat [fíːt]	偉業				1816
temperament [témpərəmənt]	気質				1817
chill [tʃíl]	寒気				1818
appliance [əpláiəns]	器具				1819
predecessor [prédisesər]	前任				1820

4
Final

139

No.	英語フレーズ	フレーズ書きこみ	日本語フレーズ
1821	a child as a separate entity		独立した存在としての子供
1822	receive warm hospitality		あたたかいもてなしを受ける
1823	a narrative of his journey		彼の旅行の話
1824	a small segment of the population		住民のほんの一部分
1825	prevent a catastrophe		大災害を防止する
1826	the British monarch		イギリスの君主
1827	due to time constraints		時間的制約があるので
1828	an amendment to the law		法律の改正
1829	the structure of the cosmos		宇宙の構造
1830	walk *down* the aisle		通路を歩く
1831	the top of the hierarchy		階級制度の頂点
1832	an expressway toll		高速道路の通行料
1833	a transaction with the company		その会社との取引
1834	A burglar broke into the house.		その家に強盗が入った
1835	put up with tyranny		圧政に耐える
1836	an animal parasite		動物寄生生物
1837	women's intuition		女の直感
1838	former communist countries		元共産主義の国々
1839	a legacy of the Renaissance		ルネサンスの遺産
1840	the veins in the forehead		額の静脈
1841	a discourse on politics		政治についての論説
1842	dairy *products*		乳製品
1843	Asian art and artifacts		アジアの美術と工芸品
1844	an outlet for frustration		欲求不満のはけ口
1845	watch with apprehension		不安そうに見つめる
1846	a mood of melancholy		憂うつな気分
1847	the quest for novelty		目新しさの追求
1848	a specimen of a rare plant		珍しい植物の標本
1849	good hygiene practices		よい衛生習慣
1850	use guerrilla tactics		ゲリラ戦術を使う

⑵名詞：本冊 p. 296 ～ 299

単語	意味	書きこみ①	書きこみ②	書きこみ③	No.
entity [éntəti]	存在				1821
hospitality [hɑspitǽləti]	もてなし				1822
narrative [nǽrətiv]	話				1823
segment [ségmənt]	部分				1824
catastrophe [kətǽstrəfi]	大災害				1825
monarch [mánərk]	君主				1826
constraint [kənstréint]	制約				1827
amendment [əméndmənt]	改正				1828
cosmos [kázməs]	宇宙				1829
aisle [áil]	通路				1830
hierarchy [háiərɑːrki]	階級制度				1831
toll [tóul]	通行料				1832
transaction [trænsǽkʃən]	取引				1833
burglar [bɔ́ːrɡlər]	強盗				1834
tyranny [tírəni]	圧政				1835
parasite [pǽrəsait]	寄生生物				1836
intuition [intʲu(ː)íʃən]	直感				1837
communist [kámjənist]	共産主義者				1838
legacy [léɡəsi]	遺産				1839
vein [véin]	静脈				1840
discourse [dískɔːrs]	論説				1841
dairy [déəri]	乳製品				1842
artifact [áːrtifækt]	工芸品				1843
outlet [áutlet]	はけ口				1844
apprehension [æprihénʃən]	不安				1845
melancholy [mélənkɑli]	憂うつ				1846
novelty [návəlti]	目新しさ				1847
specimen [spésəmin]	標本				1848
hygiene [háidʒiːn]	衛生				1849
tactics [tǽktiks]	戦術				1850

4

Final

No.	英語フレーズ	フレーズ書きこみ	日本語フレーズ
1851	a monopoly on the tea market		茶の市場の独占
1852	as a token of our friendship		我々の友情の印として
1853	the English aristocracy		イギリスの貴族階級
1854	*take* revenge *on* an enemy		敵に復讐する
1855	a human rights activist		人権活動家
1856	empty rhetoric		中身のない美辞麗句
1857	a successful entrepreneur		成功した起業家
1858	take a census every ten years		10年毎に国勢調査をおこなう
1859	be *on the* verge *of* extinction		絶滅の瀬戸際にいる
1860	the advent *of* the Internet		インターネットの出現
1861	an analogy between the heart and a pump		心臓とポンプの類似点
1862	irrigation systems		かんがいシステム
1863	media coverage of the accident		メディアによるその事故の報道
1864	traditional French cuisine		伝統的なフランス料理
1865	a menace to world peace		世界平和に対する脅威
1866	the perils of the road		道路の危険
1867	have long limbs		手足が長い
1868	assault *on* the enemy's base		敵基地への攻撃
1869	hatred of war		戦争に対する憎しみ
1870	patient autonomy		患者の自主性
1871	go to cram *school*		塾に通う
1872	a government subsidy		政府の補助金
1873	empathy *for* others		他者への共感
1874	slang expressions		俗語表現
1875	maintain good posture		よい姿勢を保つ
1876	a political ideology		政治的なイデオロギー
1877	Wealth can be a curse.		富は災いのもとになりうる
1878	have a brain tumor		脳腫瘍がある
1879	turn right *at* the intersection		交差点で右に曲がる
1880	the duration of the contract		契約の期間

単語	意味	書きこみ①	書きこみ②	書きこみ③	No.
monopoly [mənápəli]	独占				1851
token [tóukn]	印				1852
aristocracy [æristάkrəsi]	貴族階級				1853
revenge [rivéndʒ]	復讐				1854
activist [ǽktivist]	活動家				1855
rhetoric [rétərik]	美辞麗句				1856
entrepreneur [ɑ:ntrəprənə́:r]	起業家				1857
census [sénsəs]	国勢調査				1858
verge [və́:rdʒ]	瀬戸際				1859
advent [ǽdvent]	出現				1860
analogy [ənǽlədʒi]	類似点				1861
irrigation [irigéiʃən]	かんがい				1862
coverage [kʌ́vəridʒ]	報道				1863
cuisine [kwizí:n]	料理				1864
menace [ménəs]	脅威				1865
peril [pérəl]	危険				1866
limb [lím]	手足				1867
assault [əsɔ́:lt]	攻撃				1868
hatred [héitrid]	憎しみ				1869
autonomy [ɔ:tánəmi]	自主性				1870
cram [krǽm]	塾				1871
subsidy [sʌ́bsədi]	補助金				1872
empathy [émpəθi]	共感				1873
slang [slǽŋ]	俗語				1874
posture [pάstʃər]	姿勢				1875
ideology [aidiάlədʒi]	イデオロギー				1876
curse [kə́:rs]	災いのもと				1877
tumor [tjú:mər]	腫瘍				1878
intersection [intərsékʃən]	交差点				1879
duration [djuəréiʃən]	期間				1880

4 Final

No.	英語フレーズ	フレーズ書きこみ	日本語フレーズ
1881	deforestation in the Amazon		アマゾンの森林破壊
1882	take precautions against fires		火事に用心する
1883	a bunch of flowers		ひとたばの花
1884	put up with her shortcomings		彼女の欠点を我慢する
1885	aspirations to be an artist		芸術家になりたいという熱望
1886	psychologists and psychiatrists		心理学者と精神科医
1887	packaging and shipping		包装と発送
1888	a United States Senator		合衆国上院議員
1889	an international statesman		国際的な政治家
1890	instruct a subordinate		部下に指示する
1891	fill a vacuum		空白を埋める
1892	the quest *for* the truth		真理の探究
1893	Buddhist meditation		仏教の瞑想
1894	subscribers to the service		その事業の加入者
1895	solve a riddle		謎を解く
1896	be dressed in rags		ぼろを着ている
1897	be covered with rust		さびで覆われる
1898	public sanitation		公衆衛生
1899	*in the* midst *of* the lecture		授業のまっただ中に
1900	childhood mischief		子供時代のいたずら
1901	an English proficiency test		英語検定試験
1902	have no recollection of the past		過去の記憶がない
1903	38 degrees north latitude		北緯38度
1904	friction *between* the two countries		二国間の摩擦
1905	Botanists study plants.		植物学者は植物を研究する
1906	Mendel's laws of heredity		メンデルの遺伝の法則
1907	contempt *for* authority		権威に対する軽蔑
1908	the anatomy of the human brain		ヒトの脳の構造
1909	a man of integrity		誠実な人
1910	a cargo ship		貨物船

単語	意味	書きこみ①	書きこみ②	書きこみ③	No.
deforestation [diːfɔ(ː)ristéiʃən]	森林破壊				1881
precaution [prikɔ́ːʃən]	用心				1882
bunch [bʌ́ntʃ]	たば				1883
shortcoming [ʃɔ́ːrtkʌmiŋ]	欠点				1884
aspiration [æspəréiʃən]	熱望				1885
psychiatrist [saikáiətrist]	精神科医				1886
shipping [ʃípiŋ]	発送				1887
senator [sénətər]	上院議員				1888
statesman [stéitsmən]	政治家				1889
subordinate [səbɔ́ːrdənət]	部下				1890
vacuum [vǽkjuəm]	空白				1891
quest [kwést]	探究				1892
meditation [meditéiʃən]	瞑想				1893
subscriber [səbskráibər]	加入者				1894
riddle [rídl]	謎				1895
rag [rǽg]	ぼろ				1896
rust [rʌ́st]	さび				1897
sanitation [sænətéiʃən]	衛生				1898
midst [mídst]	まっただ中				1899
mischief [místʃif]	いたずら				1900
proficiency [prəfíʃənsi]	検定				1901
recollection [rekəlékʃən]	記憶				1902
latitude [lǽtətjuːd]	緯度				1903
friction [fríkʃən]	摩擦				1904
botanist [bútənist]	植物学者				1905
heredity [hərédəti]	遺伝				1906
contempt [kəntémpt]	軽蔑				1907
anatomy [ənǽtəmi]	構造				1908
integrity [intégrəti]	誠実				1909
cargo [káːrgou]	貨物				1910

4
Final

No.	英語フレーズ	フレーズ書きこみ	日本語フレーズ
1911	*take* a bribe		わいろを受け取る
1912	a massive volcanic eruption		大規模な火山の噴火
1913	weddings and funerals		結婚式と葬式
1914	America's trade deficit		アメリカの貿易赤字
1915	*the* bulk *of* the population		人口の大部分
1916	how to marry a millionaire		百万長者と結婚する方法
1917	be burned to ashes		燃えて灰になる
1918	outside the realm of science		科学の領域外
1919	workers on banana plantations		バナナ農園の労働者
1920	a farmer with his plow		すきを持った農民
1921	buy a drink from a vending *machine*		自動販売機で飲み物を買う
1922	look after orphans		孤児の世話をする
1923	connections between neurons		ニューロン間の結合
1924	destroy the vegetation in the area		その地域の植生を破壊する
1925	a brave warrior		勇敢な戦士
1926	a genetic mutation		遺伝子の突然変異
1927	the city's sewage system		その都市の下水設備
1928	propose a new paradigm		新しい理論的枠組を提起する
1929	the Kyoto Protocol		京都議定書
1930	build a hundred-story skyscraper		100階の超高層ビルを建てる
1931	His opinion is *in* accord *with* mine.		彼の意見は私と一致する
1932	government bureaucrats		政府の官僚
1933	*a* vast array *of* spices		非常に多彩なスパイス
1934	a clash of civilizations		文明同士の衝突
1935	endure terrible torture		恐ろしい拷問に耐える
1936	Queen Victoria's reign		ヴィクトリア女王の統治
1937	a graduation thesis		卒業論文
1938	a four-digit number		4桁の数字
1939	a political agenda		政治的課題
1940	the onset of dementia		認知症の発症

単語	意味	書きこみ①	書きこみ②	書きこみ③	No.
bribe [bráib]	わいろ				1911
eruption [irʌ́pʃən]	噴火				1912
funeral [fjúːnərəl]	葬式				1913
deficit [défisit]	赤字				1914
bulk [bʌ́lk]	大部分				1915
millionaire [miljənéər]	百万長者				1916
ash [ǽʃ]	灰				1917
realm [rélm]	領域				1918
plantation [plæntéiʃən]	農園				1919
plow [pláu]	すき				1920
vending [véndiŋ]	販売				1921
orphan [ɔ́ːrfn]	孤児				1922
neuron [njúərɑn]	ニューロン				1923
vegetation [vedʒətéiʃən]	植生				1924
warrior [wɔ́(ː)riər]	戦士				1925
mutation [mjuːtéiʃən]	突然変異				1926
sewage [súːidʒ]	下水				1927
paradigm [pǽrədaim]	理論的枠組				1928
protocol [próutəkɑl]	議定書				1929
skyscraper [skáiskreipər]	超高層ビル				1930
accord [əkɔ́ːrd]	一致				1931
bureaucrat [bjúərəkræt]	官僚				1932
an array of A [əréi]	多彩なA				1933
clash [klǽʃ]	衝突				1934
torture [tɔ́ːrtʃər]	拷問				1935
reign [réin]	統治				1936
thesis [θíːsis]	論文				1937
digit [dídʒit]	桁				1938
agenda [ədʒéndə]	課題				1939
onset [ɑ́nset]	発症				1940

No.	英語フレーズ	フレーズ書きこみ	日本語フレーズ
1941	landless peasants in India		インドの土地を持たない小作農
1942	harmful ultraviolet light		有害な紫外線
1943	a world-renowned singer		世界的に有名な歌手
1944	a transparent silk nightgown		透き通った絹のナイトガウン
1945	read in dim light		薄暗い明かりで本を読む
1946	a legitimate claim		正当な要求
1947	the adverse effect of global warming		地球温暖化の悪影響
1948	a swift reaction		すばやい反応
1949	naive young people		世間知らずの若者
1950	I'm not as dumb as I look.		私は見かけほどばかではない
1951	gloomy prospccts		暗い見通し
1952	My father was furious *with* me.		父は私に激怒した
1953	make an earnest effort		まじめな努力をする
1954	What a terrific idea!		何とすばらしい考えだろう
1955	a vertical wall of rock		垂直な岩壁
1956	a wicked desire		邪悪な欲望
1957	a subjective impression		主観的な印象
1958	enlightened young people		進んだ考えの若者たち
1959	authentic Italian food		本物のイタリア料理
1960	a brutal murder		残忍な殺人事件
1961	I feel dizzy when I stand up.		立ち上がるとめまいがする
1962	sheer good luck		まったくの幸運
1963	a naughty little boy		いたずらな少年
1964	wipe with a damp towel		湿ったタオルでふく
1965	static electricity		静電気
1966	The plan *is* doomed *to* failure.		その計画は失敗する運命にある
1967	acute respiratory disease		急性呼吸器病
1968	differ in innumerable ways		無数の点で異なる
1969	my clumsy fingers		私の不器用な指
1970	aesthetic sensibility		美的感性

単語	意味	書きこみ①	書きこみ②	書きこみ③	No.
peasant [pézənt]	小作農				1941
ultraviolet [ʌltrəváiələt]	紫外線の				1942
renowned [rináund]	有名な				1943
transparent [trænspéərənt]	透き通った				1944
dim [dím]	薄暗い				1945
legitimate [lidʒítimit]	正当な				1946
adverse [ædvə́ːrs]	逆の				1947
swift [swíft]	すばやい				1948
naive [nɑːíːv]	世間知らずの				1949
dumb [dʌ́m]	ばかな				1950
gloomy [glúːmi]	暗い				1951
furious [fjúəriəs]	激怒した				1952
earnest [ə́ːrnist]	まじめな				1953
terrific [tərífik]	すばらしい				1954
vertical [və́ːrtikəl]	垂直な				1955
wicked [wíkid]	邪悪な				1956
subjective [səbdʒéktiv]	主観的な				1957
enlightened [inláitnd]	進んだ考えの				1958
authentic [ɔːθéntik]	本物の				1959
brutal [brúːtl]	残忍な				1960
dizzy [dízi]	めまいがする				1961
sheer [ʃíər]	まったくの				1962
naughty [nɔ́ːti]	いたずらな				1963
damp [dǽmp]	湿った				1964
static [stǽtik]	静的な				1965
doomed [dúːmd]	運命にある				1966
respiratory [réspərətɔːri]	呼吸器の				1967
innumerable [injúːmərəbl]	無数の				1968
clumsy [klʌ́mzi]	不器用な				1969
aesthetic [esθétik]	美的な				1970

4

Final

No.	英語フレーズ	フレーズ書きこみ	日本語フレーズ
1971	be obsessed *with* dieting		ダイエットにとりつかれている
1972	a life detached *from* the world		世間から切り離された生活
1973	a wrecked ship		難破した船
1974	his reckless driving		彼の無謀な運転
1975	his arrogant attitude		あいつのごう慢な態度
1976	be preoccupied *with* the problem		その問題で頭がいっぱいだ
1977	a gigantic spaceship		巨大な宇宙船
1978	the most conspicuous example		最も顕著な例
1979	a slender girl with long hair		長い髪のすらりとした女の子
1980	a manifest mistake		明らかな誤り
1981	keep the room tidy		部屋をきちんとしておく
1982	a skeptical view of life		懐疑的な人生観
1983	a notorious crime		悪名高い犯罪
1984	an anonymous letter		匿名の手紙
1985	a monotonous school life		単調な学校生活
1986	have ample opportunity to learn		学習する機会が豊富にある
1987	a trim appearance		こざれいな服装
1988	savage violence		野蛮な暴力
1989	a logically coherent system		論理的に一貫した制度
1990	an eloquent speech		雄弁な演説
1991	a foul-smelling gas		不快なにおいのするガス
1992	a rise in juvenile crime		青少年の犯罪の増加
1993	compulsory education		義務教育
1994	*be* prone *to* catch fire		燃えやすい
1995	an arbitrary decision		勝手な決定
1996	an ingenious design		独創的な設計
1997	the divine right of kings		神聖なる王の権利
1998	a tender smile		やさしい笑顔
1999	be outraged by his behavior		彼の振る舞いに憤慨している
2000	the intrinsic value of gold		金の本来の価値

単語	意味	書きこみ①	書きこみ②	書きこみ③	No.
obsessed [əbsést]	とりつかれている				1971 ☐
detached [ditǽtʃt]	切り離された				1972 ☐
wrecked [rékt]	難破した				1973 ☐
reckless [rékləs]	無謀な				1974 ☐
arrogant [ǽrəgənt]	ごう慢な				1975 ☐
preoccupied [priákjupaid]	頭がいっぱいで				1976 ☐
gigantic [dʒaigǽntik]	巨大な				1977 ☐
conspicuous [kənspíkjuəs]	顕著な				1978 ☐
slender [sléndər]	すらりとした				1979 ☐
manifest [mǽnifest]	明らかな				1980 ☐
tidy [táidi]	きちんと				1981 ☐
skeptical [sképtikəl]	懐疑的な				1982 ☐
notorious [noutɔ́:riəs]	悪名高い				1983 ☐
anonymous [ənániməs]	匿名の				1984 ☐
monotonous [mənátənəs]	単調な				1985 ☐
ample [ǽmpl]	豊富な				1986 ☐
trim [trím]	こぎれいな				1987 ☐
savage [sǽvidʒ]	野蛮な				1988 ☐
coherent [kouhíərənt]	一貫した				1989 ☐
eloquent [éləkwənt]	雄弁な				1990 ☐
foul [fául]	不快な				1991 ☐
juvenile [dʒú:vənail]	青少年の				1992 ☐
compulsory [kəmpʌ́lsəri]	義務的な				1993 ☐
be prone to V [próun]	Vしやすい				1994 ☐
arbitrary [ɑ́:rbitreri]	勝手な				1995 ☐
ingenious [indʒí:njəs]	独創的な				1996 ☐
divine [diváin]	神聖な				1997 ☐
tender [téndər]	やさしい				1998 ☐
outraged [áutreidʒd]	憤慨している				1999 ☐
intrinsic [intrínsik]	本来の				2000 ☐

No.	英語フレーズ	フレーズ書きこみ	日本語フレーズ
2001	be paralyzed from the waist down		下半身が麻痺している
2002	be compatible *with* their values		彼らの価値観に適合する
2003	shout patriotic slogans		愛国的なスローガンを叫ぶ
2004	an eminent scientist		名高い科学者
2005	a potent weapon		強力な武器
2006	be completely insane		完全に正気を失っている
2007	a staple food		主食
2008	secondhand smoke		間接喫煙 [副流煙]
2009	indigenous peoples of Australia		オーストラリアの先住民
2010	be of the utmost importance		最も重要である
2011	an integral *part of* society		社会の不可欠な部分
2012	intricate pattern		複雑な模様
2013	demographic changes		人口統計の変化
2014	a mighty king		強力な王
2015	The building remains intact.		その建物は無傷のままだ
2016	*be* intent *on* marrying him		彼と結婚する決意をしている
2017	a very intriguing question		非常に興味深い問題
2018	marry merry Mary		陽気なメリーと結婚する
2019	perpetual peace		永続する平和
2020	a spinal injury		脊椎のけが
2021	be susceptible to disease		病気にかかりやすい
2022	mandatory standards for safety		義務的な安全基準
2023	stand upright		まっすぐに立つ
2024	stop abruptly		不意に停止する
2025	He's a dog lover. Conversely, I'm a cat lover.		彼は犬好きだ。逆に私は猫好きだ。
2026	predominantly female jobs		主に女性の仕事
2027	He wrote it down lest he forget.		園 忘れないように彼は書き留めた

⑶形容詞, ⑷副詞：本冊 p. 317 〜 321

単語	意味	書きこみ①	書きこみ②	書きこみ③	No.
paralyzed [pǽrəlaizd]	麻痺している				2001
compatible [kəmpǽtəbl]	適合する				2002
patriotic [peitriátik]	愛国的な				2003
eminent [émineənt]	名高い				2004
potent [póutənt]	強力な				2005
insane [inséin]	正気を失っている				2006
staple [stéipl]	主な				2007
secondhand [sékəndhǽnd]	間接的な				2008
indigenous [indídʒənəs]	先住の				2009
utmost [ʌ́tmoust]	最も				2010
integral [íntegrəl]	不可欠な				2011
intricate [íntrikit]	複雑な				2012
demographic [deməɡrǽfik]	人口統計の				2013
mighty [máiti]	強力な				2014
intact [intǽkt]	無傷の				2015
intent [intént]	決意をしている				2016
intriguing [intríːɡiŋ]	興味深い				2017
merry [méri]	陽気な				2018
perpetual [pərpétʃuəl]	永続する				2019
spinal [spáinl]	脊椎の				2020
susceptible [səséptəbl]	かかりやすい				2021
mandatory [mǽndətɔːri]	義務的な				2022
upright [ʌ́prait]	まっすぐに				2023
abruptly [əbrʌ́ptli]	不意に				2024
conversely [kənvə́ːrsli]	逆に				2025
predominantly [pridámineəntli]	主に				2026
lest [lést]	接 〜しないように				2027

4

Final

Stage 5

多義語の Brush Up

"All's well that ends well."

* * *

終わりよければすべてよし。

No.	英語フレーズ	フレーズ書きこみ	日本語フレーズ
1	run a big company		動 大会社を経営する
2-1	meet people's needs		動 人々の必要を満たす
2-2	how to meet the problem		動 問題に対処する方法
3-1	the right to vote		名 投票する権利
3-2	right and wrong		名 善と悪
3-3	right in front of my house		副 私の家のすぐ前に
4-1	The war lasted four years.		動 戦争は4年続いた
4-2	Our food will last a week.		動 食料は一週間持つだろう
4-3	the last man who would tell a lie		形 最もうそをつきそうにない人
4-4	He's moved twice in *the* last year.		形 彼は最近1年間に2回引っ越した
5	I *can't* stand this heat.		動 この暑さには耐えられない
6-1	Now it's your turn.		名 さあ君の番だ
6-2	the turn of the century		名 世紀の変わり目
7-1	It is also *the* case *with* him.		名 それは彼についても事実だ
7-2	a murder case		名 殺人事件
7-3	make a case *for* war		名 戦争を支持する主張をする
7-4	new cases of malaria		名 マラリアの新しい患者
8-1	face a problem		動 問題に直面する
8-2	problems facing Japan		動 日本に迫っている問題
8-3	lose face		名 面目を失う
9-1	a certain amount of time		形 ある程度の時間
9-2	I am certain *of* his success.		形 私は彼の成功を確信している
9-3	He is certain to come.		形 彼が来るのは確実だ
10-1	keep bad company		名 悪い仲間とつきあう
10-2	I enjoy your company.		名 君と一緒にいることは楽しい
10-3	We have company today.		名 今日は来客がある
11-1	attend the meeting		動 ミーティングに出席する
11-2	attend to patients		動 患者を世話する
11-3	attend *to* what he says		動 彼の言うことに注意する

No.	英語フレーズ	フレーズ書きこみ	日本語フレーズ
12-1	He worked hard; otherwise he would have failed.		副 彼は努力した。さもなければ失敗しただろう。
12-2	He is poor but otherwise happy.		副 彼は貧しいがその他の点では幸福だ
12-3	He is honest, but people think otherwise.		副 彼は正直なのに人はちがうと思っている
12-4	I can't do it otherwise.		副 ちがう方法ではできない
13-1	miss the last train		動 終電車に乗り遅れる
13-2	I sometimes miss Japan.		動 時には日本が恋しい
13-3	You can't miss it.		動 見逃すはずないよ
14-1	use scientific terms		名 科学用語を使う
14-2	long-term planning		名 長期的な計画
14-3	I am *on* good terms *with* him.		名 彼とは仲がよい
15-1	theory and practice		名 理論と実践
15-2	business practice		名 商習慣
15-3	practice medicine		動 医者を営む
16-1	face a new challenge		名 新しい難問に直面する
16-2	challenge the theory		動 その理論に異議をとなえる
17	a race problem		名 人種問題
18-1	a political issue		名 政治問題
18-2	issue an order		動 命令を出す
18-3	the latest issue of *Time*		名 「タイム」の最新号
19-1	the Democratic Party		名 民主党
19-2	a party of tourists		名 観光客の一団
19-3	Your party is on the line.		名 相手の方が電話に出ています
20	There is no room for doubt.		名 疑問の余地はない
21-1	In a sense, it is right.		名 ある意味ではそれは正しい
21-2	He *came to his* senses.		名 彼は正気に戻った
22-1	This pen *will* do.		動 このペンで十分役に立つ
22-2	do harm *to* the area		動 その地域に害を与える
23-1	*play* a part *in* the economy		名 経済で役割を果たす
23-2	a fault *on* our part		名 私たちの側の過失
23-3	part *with* the car		動 車を手放す

5 多義語

No.	英語フレーズ	フレーズ書きこみ	日本語フレーズ
24-1 ☐	Tell me the exact figures.		名 正確な数字を教えてくれ
24-2 ☐	historical figures		名 歴史上の人物
24-3 ☐	She has a beautiful figure.		名 彼女はスタイルが美しい
24-4 ☐	I figure you are busy.		動 君は忙しいと思う
25-1 ☐	his true character		名 彼の本当の性格
25-2 ☐	He's an odd character.		名 彼は変わった人物だ
25-3 ☐	the characters in the novel		名 その小説の登場人物
26 ☐	*the* very man I was looking for		形 私が探していたまさにその男
27-1 ☐	order a book *from* England		動 英国に本を注文する
27-2 ☐	carry out his order		名 彼の命令を遂行する
27-3 ☐	law and order		名 法と秩序
27-4 ☐	in alphabetical order		名 アルファベット順で
28-1 ☐	That sounds true.		動 それは本当らしく聞こえる
28-2 ☐	a sound body		形 健全な肉体
28-3 ☐	She is sound *asleep*.		副 彼女はぐっすり眠っている
29-1 ☐	*In* some ways they are right.		名 いくつかの点で彼らは正しい
29-2 ☐	The island is a long way off.		名 その島までは距離が遠い
29-3 ☐	Come this way, please.		名 こちらの方へどうぞ
30-1 ☐	concern *about* the future		名 将来への不安
30-2 ☐	concern *for* others		名 他人への思いやり
30-3 ☐	This problem concerns everyone.		動 この問題はみんなに関係する
30-4 ☐	a matter *of* great concern		名 大変重要な問題
31 ☐	This is even better.		副 これはさらによい
32-1 ☐	He is still working.		副 まだ彼は働いている
32-2 ☐	a still better idea		副 さらによい考え
32-3 ☐	The water became still.		形 水は静かになった
32-4 ☐	It's raining. Still, I have to go.		副 雨だ。それでも行かねばならない。
33-1 ☐	I meant *to* call you sooner.		動 すぐに電話するつもりだった
33-2 ☐	I love you. I mean it.		動 好きだ。本気で言ってるんだ。
33-3 ☐	He is mean to me.		形 彼は私に意地悪だ

No.	英語フレーズ	フレーズ書きこみ	日本語フレーズ
34-1	leave an umbrella on the train		動 電車に傘を置き忘れる
34-2	leave the door open		動 ドアを開けたまま放置する
34-3	There is little time left.		動 残り時間はほとんどない
34-4	take paid parental leave		名 有給の育児休暇を取る
35-1	Most people think so.		形 たいていの人はそう考える
35-2	a most important point		副 非常に重要な点
36	Things have changed.		名 状況は変わった
37-1	against his will		名 彼の意志に反して
37-2	leave a will		名 遺言を残す
38-1	an excited state of mind		名 興奮した精神状態
38-2	state an opinion		動 意見を述べる
38-3	a state secret		名 国家の機密
39-1	I *don't* mind walk*ing*.		動 歩くのはいやではない
39-2	talented minds		名 才能ある人々
40	I *cannot* help laugh*ing*.		動 笑わずにはいられない
41-1	It *doesn't* matter what he says.		動 彼が何と言おうと重要ではない
41-2	soft matter		名 やわらかい物質
41-3	Something *is the* matter *with* my car.		名 私の車はどこか異常だ
42-1	a means of communication		名 コミュニケーションの手段
42-2	a man of means		名 資産家
43-1	the contents of her letter		名 彼女の手紙の内容
43-2	be content *with* the result		形 結果に満足している
44-1	in some respects		名 いくつかの点で
44-2	respect the law		動 法を尊重する
45-1	the ability to reason		動 推理する能力
45-2	He lost all reason.		名 彼はすっかり理性を失った
46-1	the cause of the failure		名 失敗の原因
46-2	cause a lot of trouble		動 多くの問題を引き起こす
46-3	advance the cause of peace		名 平和運動を推進する

5

多義語

No.	英語フレーズ	フレーズ書きこみ	日本語フレーズ
47-1	hold a meeting		動 会合を開く
47-2	They hold that the earth is flat.		動 彼らは地球は平らだと考える
48-1	make a fortune in oil		名 石油で財産を築く
48-2	bring *good* fortune		名 幸運をもたらす
49-1	the future of humanity		名 人類の未来
49-2	science and *the* humanities		名 自然科学と人文科学
50	a means to an end		名 目的を果たす手段
51-1	form a new company		動 新しい会社を作る
51-2	*fill out* the application form		名 申込用紙に記入する
51-3	Knowledge is a form *of* power.		名 知識は一種の力だ
52-1	I have no change with me.		名 小銭の持ち合わせがない
52-2	Keep the change.		名 おつりはいりません
53-1	my present address		形 現在の住所
53-2	*the* present and future		名 現在と未来
53-3	the people present		形 出席している人々
53-4	present a plan *to* the president		動 社長に計画を提示する
53-5	present Mr. Boyd *to* you		動 君にボイド氏を紹介する
53-6	present the winner *with* the prize		動 勝者に賞を与える
54-1	works of art		名 芸術作品
54-2	This plan will work.		動 この計画はうまく行く
55-1	One thing leads *to* another.		動 ひとつの事が別の事を引き起こす
55-2	lead a happy *life*		動 幸福な生活を送る
55-3	leading artists		形 一流のアーティスト
56	There is no life on the moon.		名 月には生物がいない
57-1	I *don't* care what you say.		動 君が何と言おうと気にしない
57-2	A baby requires constant care.		名 赤ちゃんはつねに世話が必要だ
58-1	middle-class families		名 中流階級の家庭
58-2	sleep *in* class		名 授業中にいねむりする
59	his natural abilities		形 彼の生まれながらの才能

No.	英語フレーズ	フレーズ書きこみ	日本語フレーズ
60-1	a life free *from* stress		形 ストレスの無い生活
60-2	free them *from* work		動 彼らを労働から解放する
61-1	head straight *for* Paris		動 まっすぐパリに向かう
61-2	a team headed by a woman		動 女性に率いられたチーム
62-1	deal *with* the problem		動 問題を処理する
62-2	*a great* deal of data		名 大量のデータ
62-3	*make* a deal *with* Microsoft		名 マイクロソフトと取引する
63-1	my view *of* education		名 教育に関する私の見解
63-2	view Japan *as* a safe society		動 日本を安全な社会と考える
64	the chance *of* making them angry		名 彼らを怒らせる可能性
65-1	very close *to* the city		形 都市にとても近い
65-2	a close friend		形 親しい友達
65-3	a close examination		形 綿密な検査
65-4	the close of the 20th century		名 20世紀の終わり
66-1	protect workers' interests		名 労働者の利益を守る
66-2	lend money at high interest rates		名 高い利率で金を貸す
67	fail *to* understand him		動 彼を理解できない
68-1	a major problem		形 主要な問題
68-2	major *in* economics		動 経済学を専攻する
69-1	agree *to* his proposal		動 彼の提案に同意する
69-2	I agree *with* you.		動 私も君と同じ考えである
70-1	British colonial rule		名 イギリスの植民地支配
70-2	Small families are *the* rule in Japan.		名 日本では小家族が普通だ
71-1	the process of thought		名 思考の過程
71-2	how to process meat		動 肉を加工する方法
71-3	process data with a computer		動 コンピュータでデータを処理する
72-1	a large amount of water		名 大量の水
72-2	The expenses amount *to* $90.		動 経費は合計90ドルになる
72-3	This act amounts *to* stealing.		動 この行為は盗みに等しい

5

多義語

No.	英語フレーズ	フレーズ書きこみ	日本語フレーズ
73 ☐	long *for* world peace		動 世界平和を切望する
74-1 ☐	The line is busy.		名 電話が話し中だ
74-2 ☐	wait *in* line		名 1列に並んで待つ
74-3 ☐	*drop* him a line		名 彼に短い手紙を書く
74-4 ☐	this line *of business*		名 こういう種類の仕事
75 ☐	a word of six letters		名 6文字の単語
76-1 ☐	People are subject *to* the law.		形 人は法に支配される
76-2 ☐	I am subject *to* illness.		形 私は病気にかかりやすい
76-3 ☐	Let's change the subject.		名 話題を変えよう
76-4 ☐	My favorite subject is math.		名 好きな学科は数学です
76-5 ☐	the subject of the experiment		名 その実験の被験者
77-1 ☐	*the* rest of his life		名 彼の残りの人生
77-2 ☐	Let's take a rest.		名 休息をとろう
78-1 ☐	the fine *for* speeding		名 スピード違反の罰金
78-2 ☐	be fined $60		動 60ドルの罰金を科される
78-3 ☐	fine sand on the beach		形 海岸の細かい砂
79 ☐	My shoes have worn thin.		動 靴がすり減って薄くなった
80-1 ☐	Please remember me *to* your wife.		動 奥さんによろしく伝えてください
80-2 ☐	remember *to* lock the door		動 忘れずにドアにカギをかける
81-1 ☐	The insurance covers the cost.		動 保険で費用をまかなう
81-2 ☐	cover the big news		動 大ニュースを報道[取材]する
81-3 ☐	cover 120 miles an hour		動 1時間に120マイル進む
82 ☐	book a flight		動 飛行機を予約する
83 ☐	store information in a computer		動 コンピュータに情報を蓄える
84-1 ☐	save money for a new house		動 新しい家のためお金を蓄える
84-2 ☐	save time and trouble		動 時間と手間を省く
84-3 ☐	answer all the questions save one		前 1つを除きすべての質問に答える
85-1 ☐	serve good food		動 うまい料理を出す
85-2 ☐	serve many purposes		動 多くの目的に役立つ
85-3 ☐	serve the king		動 王に仕える

No.	英語フレーズ	フレーズ書きこみ	日本語フレーズ
86-1	Black people account *for* 10% of the population.		動 黒人が人口の10%を占める
86-2	This accounts *for* the failure.		動 これが失敗の原因だ
86-3	account *for* the difference		動 違いを説明する
87	the art of writing		名 書く技術
88-1	He was fired *from* his job.		動 彼は仕事をクビになった
88-2	fire into the crowd		動 群衆に向かって発砲する
89-1	a strange flying object		名 奇妙な飛行物体
89-2	an object of study		名 研究の対象
89-3	object *to* his drink*ing*		動 彼が酒を飲むのに反対する
90-1	manage *to* catch the train		動 なんとか列車に間に合う
90-2	manage a big company		動 大会社を経営する
91	*On* what grounds do you say that?		名 どんな根拠でそう言うのか
92-1	assume that money can buy happiness		動 金で幸福が買えると思い込む
92-2	assume responsibility		動 責任を引き受ける
93-1	direct contact		形 直接の接触
93-2	direct his attention *to* the fact		動 その事実に彼の注意を向ける
93-3	direct her *to* the station		動 彼女に駅への道を教える
93-4	direct the workers		動 労働者たちに指図する
94-1	If he fails, it'll be *my* fault.		名 彼が失敗したら私の責任だ
94-2	He has a lot of faults.		名 彼は欠点が多い
95-1	He is tired due *to* lack of sleep.		形 彼は睡眠不足のせいで疲れている
95-2	pay due respect		形 十分な敬意を払う
95-3	The train is due *to* arrive at ten.		形 その列車は10時に着く予定だ
95-4	The report is due next Wednesday.		形 レポートは水曜が期限だ
96-1	*in* a scientific manner		名 科学的な方法で
96-2	her friendly manner		名 彼女の好意的な態度
96-3	It's bad manners to spit.		名 つばを吐くのは行儀が悪い
97	a pretty long time		副 かなり長い間

| 1回目 | ／ | 2回目 | ／ | 3回目 | ／ |

No.	英語フレーズ	フレーズ書きこみ	日本語フレーズ
98-1	The man struck me *as* strange.		動 その男は私に奇妙な印象を与えた
98-2	Suddenly an idea struck him.		動 突然彼にある考えが浮かんだ
98-3	The typhoon struck Osaka.		動 その台風は大阪を襲った
99-1	*get* regular exercise		名 規則的に運動する
99-2	exercise power over people		動 人々に対し権力を用いる
100-1	maintain health		動 健康を維持する
100-2	maintain that he is innocent		動 彼の無罪を主張する
101-1	work for a big firm		名 大きな会社に勤める
101-2	a firm belief		形 堅い信念
102-1	a newspaper article		名 新聞の記事
102-2	an article for sale		名 販売用の品物
103	That's what counts.		動 それが重要なことだ
104-1	appreciate his talent		動 彼の才能を高く評価する
104-2	appreciate music		動 音楽を鑑賞する
104-3	I appreciate your help.		動 君の助けに感謝する
105-1	take strong measures		名 強硬な手段を用いる
105-2	a measure of respect		名 ある程度の尊敬
106-1	have a good command of English		名 英語をうまくあやつる能力がある
106-2	The hill commands a fine view.		動 丘からいい景色を見わたせる
106-3	command great respect		動 大いに尊敬を集める
107-1	bear the pain		動 痛みに耐える
107-2	bear a child		動 子供を産む
107-3	bear relation to the matter		動 その問題に関係を持つ
108-1	stick *to* the schedule		動 予定を守る
108-2	get stuck on a crowded train		動 混んだ列車で動けなくなる
108-3	stick out the tongue		動 舌を突き出す
108-4	The song stuck in my mind.		動 その歌は私の心に残った
109-1	a fixed point		動 固定された点
109-2	fix a broken car		動 壊れた車を修理する
109-3	I'll fix you a drink.		動 飲み物を作ってあげる

No.	英語フレーズ	フレーズ書きこみ	日本語フレーズ
110-1 ☐	*in* a similar fashion		名 同じようなやり方で
110-2 ☐	fashion a new world		動 新しい世界を作る
111-1 ☐	free of charge		名 料金不要で
111-2 ☐	charge a high price		動 高い代金を請求する
111-3 ☐	He is *in* charge *of* the case.		名 彼がその事件の担当だ
111-4 ☐	be charged *with* murder		動 殺人で告訴される
112-1 ☐	observe the comet		動 彗星を観察する
112-2 ☐	observe that prices would fall		動 物価は下がると述べる
112-3 ☐	observe the rule		動 規則を守る
113-1 ☐	conduct an experiment		動 実験を行う
113-2 ☐	the standards of conduct		名 行動の基準
113-3 ☐	conduct electricity		動 電気を伝える
114-1 ☐	I'll keep *my* word.		名 私は約束を守る
114-2 ☐	Could I *have a* word *with* you?		名 ちょっと話があるんですが
115-1 ☐	*get in* touch *with* him by phone		名 電話で彼に連絡をとる
115-2 ☐	The story touched him deeply.		動 その話は彼を深く感動させた
115-3 ☐	add *a* touch *of* spice		名 スパイスを少し加える
116-1 ☐	agree *to* some degree		名 ある程度まで同意する
116-2 ☐	get a master's degree		名 修士の学位を取る
117 ☐	learn a lesson from the failure		名 失敗から教訓を学ぶ
118-1 ☐	deny the existence of God		動 神の存在を否定する
118-2 ☐	deny them their civil rights		動 彼らに市民権を与えない
119 ☐	take a break for a cup of tea		名 一休みしてお茶を飲む
120 ☐	the nature of language		名 言語の本質
121-1 ☐	a letter addressed to him		動 彼に宛てられた手紙
121-2 ☐	address climate change		動 気候変動に取り組む
121-3 ☐	address the audience		動 聴衆に呼びかける
121-4 ☐	the opening address		名 開会の演説
122-1 ☐	the freedom of *the* press		名 出版の自由
122-2 ☐	be pressed for time		動 時間が切迫している

No.	英語フレーズ	フレーズ書きこみ	日本語フレーズ
123-1 ☐	an expensive item		名 高価な品物
123-2 ☐	the top news item		名 トップニュースの記事
124-1 ☐	feel pity *for* the victims		名 犠牲者に同情する
124-2 ☐	It's *a* pity that he can't come.		名 彼が来られないのは残念なことだ
125 ☐	beat the champion		動 チャンピオンに勝つ
126-1 ☐	point *out* that it is wrong		動 それは誤りだと指摘する
126-2 ☐	There's no point *in* writing it.		名 それを書く意味はない
126-3 ☐	prove his point		名 彼の主張を証明する
127-1 ☐	I lived there once.		副 私はかつてそこに住んでいた
127-2 ☐	Once she arrives, we can start.		接 彼女が来るとすぐ我々は出発できる
128-1 ☐	a healthy diet		名 健康的な食事
128-2 ☐	She is *on* a diet.		名 彼女は食事制限をしている
128-3 ☐	a member of *the* Diet		名 国会議員
129 ☐	write a paper on economics		名 経済学の論文を書く
130-1 ☐	cash a check		名 小切手を現金に換える
130-2 ☐	a dinner check		名 ディナーの勘定書
130-3 ☐	check bags at the airport		動 空港でバッグを預ける
131 ☐	Meg is a bright girl.		形 メグは賢い子だ
132-1 ☐	a sort of bird		名 一種の鳥
132-2 ☐	sort papers by date		動 日付で書類を分類する
133 ☐	The case went to court.		名 その事件は裁判になった
134-1 ☐	He *is* bound *to* fail.		形 彼はきっと失敗する
134-2 ☐	The plane *is* bound *for* Guam.		形 その飛行機はグアム行きだ
134-3 ☐	be bound by the law		動 法律に縛られる
135-1 ☐	a flat surface		形 平らな表面
135-2 ☐	live in a flat in London		名 ロンドンのアパートに住む
136-1 ☐	have no spare money		形 余分なお金はない
136-2 ☐	spare him a few minutes		動 彼のために少し時間を割く
136-3 ☐	spare him the trouble		動 彼の面倒を省く
136-4 ☐	spare *no* effort to help her		動 彼女を助ける努力を惜しまない

No.	英語フレーズ	フレーズ書きこみ	日本語フレーズ
137-1	the capital of Australia		名 オーストラリアの首都
137-2	labor and capital		名 労働と資本
138	speak in a foreign tongue		名 外国の言葉でしゃべる
139-1	credit for the discovery		名 その発見の功績
139-2	college credits		名 大学の単位
140	succeed *to* the crown		動 王位を受け継ぐ
141-1	settle the dispute		動 紛争を解決する
141-2	settle in America		動 アメリカに定住する
141-3	get married and settle *down*		動 結婚して落ち着く
142-1	a vision of the city		名 その都市の未来像
142-2	a leader of vision		名 先見の明のある指導者
142-3	have poor vision		名 視力が弱い
143-1	I have but one question.		副 1つだけ質問がある
143-2	They *all* went out but me.		前 私を除いて皆出かけた
144-1	in a given situation		形 ある特定の状況で
144-2	given the present conditions		前 現状を考慮すると
144-3	given *that* you are young		接 君が若いことを考慮すると
145-1	equal pay for equal work		名 同じ仕事に対する同じ給料
145-2	Honesty doesn't always pay.		動 正直は割に合うとは限らない
146-1	*a* good many people		形 かなり多くの人
146-2	work for the public good		名 公共の利益のために働く
147-1	teach students discipline		名 学生に規律を教える
147-2	scientists of many disciplines		名 いろんな分野の科学者たち
148-1	an electricity bill		名 電気代の請求書
148-2	a ten dollar bill		名 10ドル紙幣
148-3	pass a bill		名 法案を可決する
149-1	breathe a sigh of relief		名 安心してため息をつく
149-2	relief from poverty		名 貧困に対する救済
149-3	relief from stress		名 ストレスの除去

No.	英語フレーズ	フレーズ書きこみ	日本語フレーズ
150-1	board a plane		動 飛行機に乗り込む
150-2	the school board		名 教育委員会
151	She *got* mad at me.		形 彼女は私に腹を立てた
152-1	yield food and wood		動 食料や木材を産出する
152-2	yield *to* pressure		動 圧力に屈する
152-3	Radio yielded *to* television.		動 ラジオはテレビに取って代わられた
153-1	a rear seat		名 後部座席
153-2	rear three children		動 3人の子供を育てる
154-1	fancy restaurant		形 高級レストラン
154-2	fancy myself a novelist		動 自分が小説家だと想像する
155-1	feel no shame		名 恥と思わない
155-2	What *a* shame!		名 なんと残念なことか
156-1	waste money		動 お金を浪費する
156-2	industrial waste		名 産業廃棄物
157-1	drive the dog *away*		動 犬を追い払う
157-2	be driven by curiosity		動 好奇心に駆りたてられる
157-3	my strong drive to succeed		名 成功したいという強い欲求
158	English with an Italian accent		名 イタリアなまりの英語
159	He will make a good teacher.		動 彼はよい教師になるだろう
160-1	in his late thirties		形 彼の30代の終わりごろに
160-2	*the* late Mr. Ford		形 故フォード氏
161-1	her body and soul		名 彼女の肉体と魂
161-2	There was *not a* soul there.		名 そこには1人もいなかった
162	arms control		名 軍備制限
163-1	virtue and vice		名 美徳と悪徳
163-2	vice president		形 副大統領
164	a five-story building		名 5階建ての建物
165	She was moved by my story.		動 彼女は私の話に感動した
166-1	a parking lot		名 駐車場
166-2	She accepted her lot.		名 彼女は運命を受け入れた

No.	英語フレーズ	フレーズ書きこみ	日本語フレーズ
167-1	teach the dolphin new tricks		名 イルカに新しい芸を教える
167-2	a trick for memorizing words		名 単語を覚えるコツ
167-3	*play* a trick *on* the teacher		名 先生にいたずらする
167-4	trick him *into* buying the pot		動 彼をだましてそのつぼを買わせる
167-5	a clever trick		名 巧妙なたくらみ
168	New companies will spring up there.		動 そこに新しい会社が出現するだろう
169-1	pose a problem		動 問題を引き起こす
169-2	pose a question		動 疑問を提起する
170-1	The water is fit *to* drink.		形 その水は飲むのに適する
170-2	go to the gym to keep fit		形 健康でいるためにジムに通う
171-1	take notes on what you hear		名 聞くことをメモする
171-2	He noted that America is a big country.		動 アメリカは大国だと彼は書いた
171-3	Note that the book is non-fiction.		動 その本は実話だということに注意しなさい
171-4	He is noted *for* his intelligence.		形 彼は知的なことで有名だ
171-5	a ten-pound note		名 10ポンド紙幣
172-1	gun control laws		名 銃規制法
172-2	control group		名 実験の対照群
173-1	the school authorities		名 学校当局
173-2	the authority of the state		名 国家の権力
173-3	an authority *on* biology		名 生物学の権威
174-1	Consider a fruit, say, an orange.		フルーツ, たとえばオレンジを考えよ
174-2	Let's say you have a million dollars.		君が100万ドル持っていると仮定しよう
174-3	What do you say to go*ing* on a trip?		旅に出かけたらどうですか
175	She is fast *asleep*.		副 彼女はぐっすり眠っている
176	minute differences		形 細かい違い
177	a death sentence		名 死刑の判決
178	a gifted pianist		形 才能あるピアニスト
179	apples, peaches, *and the* like		名 リンゴや桃など
180	coin a new *term*		動 新語を作り出す

No.	英語フレーズ	フレーズ書きこみ	日本語フレーズ
181-1 ☐	She cast a spell on me.		名 彼女は私に魔法をかけた
181-2 ☐	a long dry spell		名 長い日照り続き
182 ☐	an air of confidence		名 自信がある様子
183 ☐	go hunting for big game		名 大きな獲物を狩りに行く
184-1 ☐	We've *been* conditioned *to* believe that busier is better.		動 私たちは忙しい方がよいと信じるように慣らされている
184-2 ☐	Our lives *are* conditioned *by* technology.		動 私たちの生活は技術に左右されている

ジャンル別英単語

"Words cut more than swords."

* * *

言葉は剣よりも切れる。

● 野菜・果物　ジャンル別 1 (p. 62)

No.	単語	意味	書きこみ①	書きこみ②	書きこみ③
1 ☐	**bean** [bíːn]	豆(科の植物)			
2 ☐	**cabbage** [kǽbidʒ]	キャベツ			
3 ☐	**cucumber** [kjúːkʌmbər]	キュウリ			
4 ☐	**egg plant** [ég plǽnt]	ナス			
5 ☐	**garlic** [gáːrlik]	ニンニク			
6 ☐	**ginger** [dʒíndʒər]	ショウガ			
7 ☐	**lettuce** [létəs]	レタス			
8 ☐	**pea** [píː]	(さや)エンドウ			
9 ☐	**pear** [péər]	洋ナシ			
10 ☐	**spinach** [ʒpínitʃ]	ホウレン草			
11 ☐	**squash** [skwáʃ]	カボチャ			

● 天気　ジャンル別 2 (p. 67)

No.	単語	意味	書きこみ①	書きこみ②	書きこみ③
1 ☐	**fog** [fɔ́(ː)g]	霧			
2 ☐	**frost** [frɔ́(ː)st]	霜			
3 ☐	**hail** [héil]	あられ			
4 ☐	**mist** [míst]	かすみ			
5 ☐	**shower** [ʃáuər]	にわか雨			
6 ☐	**thunder** [θʌ́ndər]	雷鳴			
7 ☐	**thunderstorm** [θʌ́ndəstɔəm]	激しい雷雨			
8 ☐	**tornado** [tɔənéidou]	竜巻			
9 ☐	**twilight** [twáilait]	夕方			

● 動物　ジャンル別 3 (p. 68)

No.	単語	意味	書きこみ①	書きこみ②	書きこみ③
1 ☐	**animal** [ǽnəml]	動物			
2 ☐	**bat** [bǽt]	コウモリ			

3 ☐	**bull** [búl]	雄牛			
4 ☐	**camel** [kǽml]	ラクダ			
5 ☐	**cow** [káu]	乳牛			
6 ☐	**deer** [díər]	シカ			
7 ☐	**donkey** [dáŋki]	ロバ			
8 ☐	**elephant** [éləfənt]	ゾウ			
9 ☐	**fox** [fáks]	キツネ			
10 ☐	**giraffe** [dʒərǽf]	キリン			
11 ☐	**goat** [góut]	ヤギ			
12 ☐	**hare** [héər]	ノウサギ			
13 ☐	**hippopotamus** [hipəpátəməs]	カバ			
14 ☐	**kitten** [kítn]	子ネコ			
15 ☐	**leopard** [lépərd]	ヒョウ			
16 ☐	**lizard** [lízərd]	トカゲ			
17 ☐	**mole** [móul]	モグラ			
18 ☐	**mouse** [máus]	ハツカネズミ			
19 ☐	**ox** [áks]	雄牛			
20 ☐	**puppy** [pʌ́pi]	子犬			
21 ☐	**rabbit** [rǽbət]	ウサギ			
22 ☐	**rat** [rǽt]	ドブネズミ			
23 ☐	**reindeer** [réindiər]	トナカイ			
24 ☐	**rhinoceros** [rainásərəs]	サイ			
25 ☐	**sea lion** [síː láiən]	アシカ			
26 ☐	**seal** [síːl]	アザラシ			
27 ☐	**sheep** [ʃíːp]	ヒツジ			
28 ☐	**snake** [snéik]	ヘビ			
29 ☐	**squirrel** [skwə́ːrəl]	リス			
30 ☐	**turtle** [tə́ːrtl]	カメ			
31 ☐	**wild boar** [wáild bɔ́ːr]	イノシシ			
32 ☐	**wolf** [wúlf]	オオカミ			
33 ☐	**zebra** [zíːbrə]	シマウマ			

ジャンル別

● 植物① 　　ジャンル別 4 　(p. 79)

No.	単語	意味	書きこみ①	書きこみ②	書きこみ③
1 ☐	**bamboo** [bæmbúː]	竹			
2 ☐	**cactus** [kǽktəs]	サボテン			
3 ☐	**cedar** [síːdə]	スギ			
4 ☐	**chestnut** [tʃésnʌt]	クリ(の木)			
5 ☐	**grass** [grǽs]	草			
6 ☐	**ivy** [áivi]	ツタ			
7 ☐	**leaf** [líːf]	葉			
8 ☐	**lily** [líli]	ユリ			
9 ☐	**maple** [méipl]	カエデ			
10 ☐	**moss** [mɔ́ːs]	コケ			
11 ☐	**oak** [óuk]	オーク			
12 ☐	**palm** [pɑ́ːm]	ヤシ			
13 ☐	**pine** [páin]	マツ			
14 ☐	**redwood** [rédwud]	セコイア			
15 ☐	**seaweed** [síːwiːd]	海藻			
16 ☐	**walnut** [wɔ́ːlnʌt]	クルミ(の木)			
17 ☐	**weed** [wíːd]	雑草			
18 ☐	**willow** [wílou]	柳			

● 虫 　　ジャンル別 5 　(p. 108)

No.	単語	意味	書きこみ①	書きこみ②	書きこみ③
1 ☐	**ant** [ǽnt]	アリ			
2 ☐	**bee** [bíː]	ハチ			
3 ☐	**beetle** [bíːtl]	カブトムシ			
4 ☐	**bug** [bʌ́g]	虫			
5 ☐	**butterfly** [bʌ́tərflai]	チョウ			
6 ☐	**caterpillar** [kǽtərpilər]	イモムシ			
7 ☐	**cicada** [səkéidə]	セミ			

No.	単語	意味	書きこみ①	書きこみ②	書きこみ③
8	cockroach [kákroutʃ]	ゴキブリ			
9	flea [flíː]	ノミ			
10	fly [flái]	ハエ			
11	mosquito [məskíːtou]	カ			
12	moth [mɔ́(ː)θ]	ガ			
13	snail [snéil]	カタツムリ			
14	spider [spáidər]	クモ			
15	wasp [wáːsp]	ジガバチ			
16	worm [wɔ́ːrm]	イモムシ			

● 鳥　　ジャンル別 6 (p. 108)

No.	単語	意味	書きこみ①	書きこみ②	書きこみ③
1	canary [kənéəri]	カナリア			
2	crow [króu]	カラス			
3	cuckoo [kúːkuː]	カッコウ			
4	dove [dʌ́v]	ハト			
5	duck [dʌ́k]	アヒル			
6	eagle [íːgl]	ワシ			
7	goose [gúːs]	ガチョウ			
8	gull [gʌ́l]	カモメ			
9	hawk [hɔ́ːk]	タカ			
10	hen [hén]	めんどり			
11	owl [ául]	フクロウ			
12	parrot [pǽrət]	オウム			
13	peacock [píːkɑk]	クジャク			
14	pigeon [pídʒən]	ハト			
15	robin [rábin]	コマドリ			
16	sparrow [spǽərou]	スズメ			
17	swallow [swálou]	ツバメ			
18	turkey [tɔ́ːrki]	七面鳥			

ジャンル別

● 図形　　ジャンル別 7 (p. 189)

No.	単語	意味	書きこみ①	書きこみ②	書きこみ③
1	**angle** [ǽngl]	角			
2	**circle** [sə́ːrkl]	円			
3	**cone** [kóun]	円すい			
4	**cube** [kjúːb]	立方体			
5	**oval** [óuvl]	卵形(の)			
6	**pentagon** [péntəgɑn]	5角形			
7	**plane** [pléin]	面			
8	**rectangle** [réktæŋgl]	長方形			
9	**side** [sáid]	辺			
10	**square** [skwéər]	正方形			
11	**triangle** [tráiæŋgl]	3角形			

● 食事　　ジャンル別 8 (p. 200)

No.	単語	意味	書きこみ①	書きこみ②	書きこみ③
1	**chopsticks** [tʃápstiks]	はし			
2	**dessert** [dizə́ːrt]	デザート			
3	**dish** [díʃ]	皿			
4	**kettle** [kétl]	やかん			
5	**lid** [líd]	ふた			
6	**mug** [mʌ́g]	マグカップ			
7	**plate** [pléit]	取り皿			
8	**saucer** [sɔ́ːsər]	受け皿			
9	**steak** [stéik]	ステーキ			
10	**stew** [stjúː]	シチュー			

● 海の生き物　ジャンル別 9 (p. 202)

No.	単語	意味	書きこみ①	書きこみ②	書きこみ③
1	a school of fish	魚の群れ			
2	cod [kάːd]	タラ			
3	dolphin [dάlfin]	イルカ			
4	jelly fish [dʒéli fiʃ]	クラゲ			
5	octopus [άktəpəs]	タコ			
6	oyster [ɔ́istər]	カキ			
7	salmon [sǽmən]	サケ			
8	sardine [sɑːrdíːn]	イワシ			
9	shark [ʃάːrk]	サメ			
10	shell [ʃél]	貝			
11	squid [skwíd]	イカ			
12	trout [tráut]	マス			
13	tuna [tjúːnə]	マグロ			
14	whale [hwéil]	クジラ			

● 人 体　ジャンル別 10 (p. 203)

No.	単語	意味	書きこみ①	書きこみ②	書きこみ③
1	ankle [ǽŋkl]	足首			
2	beard [bíərd]	あごひげ			
3	bone [bóun]	骨			
4	bowel [bául]	腸			
5	breast [brést]	胸			
6	brow [bráu]	額			
7	cheek [tʃíːk]	ほお			
8	chest [tʃést]	胸			
9	cortex [kɔ́ːrteks]	皮質			
10	elbow [élbou]	ひじ			
11	forehead [fɔ́(ː)rəd]	額			

ジャンル別

177

12 ☐	jaw [dʒɔ́ː]	あご			
13 ☐	kidney [kídni]	腎臓			
14 ☐	knee [níː]	ひざ			
15 ☐	liver [lívər]	肝臓			
16 ☐	shoulder [ʃóuldər]	肩			
17 ☐	skeleton [skélətn]	骨格			
18 ☐	skin [skín]	はだ			
19 ☐	stomach [stʌ́mək]	腹部			
20 ☐	throat [θróut]	のど			
21 ☐	toe [tóu]	足の指			
22 ☐	tooth [túːθ]	歯			
23 ☐	wrinkle [ríŋkl]	しわ			

● 衣服　ジャンル別 11 (p. 203)

No.	単語	意味	書きこみ①	書きこみ②	書きこみ③
1 ☐	blanket [blǽŋkət]	毛布			
2 ☐	collar [kálər]	えり			
3 ☐	cosmetics [kazmétiks]	化粧品			
4 ☐	cotton [kátn]	綿			
5 ☐	dye [dái]	染料			
6 ☐	feather [féðər]	羽毛			
7 ☐	fur [fɔ́ːr]	毛皮			
8 ☐	leather [léðər]	革			
9 ☐	lipstick [lípstìk]	口紅			
10 ☐	pants [pǽnts]	ズボン			
11 ☐	razor [réizər]	かみそり			
12 ☐	silk [sílk]	絹			
13 ☐	wool [wúl]	羊毛			

● 公共施設・建物　ジャンル別 12 (p. 204)

No.	単語	意味	書きこみ①	書きこみ②	書きこみ③
1	**aquarium** [əkwéəriəm]	水族館			
2	**bank** [bǽŋk]	銀行			
3	**botanical garden** [bətǽnikl gáːrdn]	植物園			
4	**church** [tʃɔ́ːrtʃ]	教会			
5	**college** [kálidʒ]	(単科)大学			
6	**dormitory** [dɔ́ːrmətɔːri]	寮			
7	**factory** [fǽktəri]	工場			
8	**gallery** [gǽləri]	美術館			
9	**garage** [gərάːdʒ]	車庫			
10	**hall** [hɔ́ːl]	会館			
11	**hospital** [háspitl]	病院			
12	**museum** [mjuːzíəm]	博物館			
13	**palace** [pǽləs]	宮殿			
14	**park** [páːrk]	公園			
15	**restaurant** [réstərənt]	レストラン			
16	**theater** [θíətər]	劇場			
17	**university** [juːnəvə́ːrsəti]	(総合)大学			

● 住　居　ジャンル別 13 (p. 204)

No.	単語	意味	書きこみ①	書きこみ②	書きこみ③
1	**apartment** [əpάːrtmənt]	アパート			
2	**backyard** [bǽkjάːrd]	裏庭			
3	**ceiling** [síːliŋ]	天井			
4	**chamber** [tʃéimbər]	小部屋			
5	**closet** [klάzət]	クローゼット			
6	**corridor** [kɔ́(ː)rədər]	ろうか			
7	**downstairs** [daunstéərz]	階下			
8	**drawer** [drɔ́ːr]	引き出し			

★
ジャンル別

179

No.	単語	意味	書きこみ①	書きこみ②	書きこみ③
9	elevator [éləveitər]	エレベーター			
10	escalator [éskəleitər]	エスカレーター			
11	gate [géit]	門			
12	rail [réil]	手すり			
13	roof [rú:f]	屋根			
14	stairs [stéərz]	階段			
15	study [stʌ́di]	書斎			
16	upstairs [ʌpstéərz]	階上			
17	wall [wɔ́:l]	壁			
18	yard [já:rd]	庭			

● 人種　ジャンル別 14 (p. 244)

No.	単語	意味	書きこみ①	書きこみ②	書きこみ③
1	Aboriginal [æbərídʒənəl]	アボリジニ			
2	African American [æfrikən əmérikən]	アフリカ系アメリカ人			
3	Anglo [ǽŋglou]	英国系米国人			
4	Anglo-Saxon [ǽŋglousǽksn]	アングロサクソン			
5	Caucasian [kɔːkéiʒən]	白人			
6	Dutch [dʌ́tʃ]	オランダ人			
7	Hispanic [hispǽnik]	ラテンアメリカ系住民			
8	Jew [dʒú:]	ユダヤ人			
9	Latino [lætí:nou]	ラテンアメリカ人			
10	Native American [néitiv əmérikən]	北米先住民			

● 職業　ジャンル別 15 (p. 245)

No.	単語	意味	書きこみ①	書きこみ②	書きこみ③
1	accountant [əkáuntənt]	会計士			
2	attendant [əténdənt]	接客係			
3	barber [bá:bə]	理髪師			
4	butcher [bútʃə]	肉屋			

No.	単語	意味	書きこみ①	書きこみ②	書きこみ③
5	carpenter [kάːpntə]	大工			
6	cashier [kæʃíə]	レジ係			
7	chairman [tʃéərmən]	議長			
8	dentist [déntəst]	歯科医			
9	director [diréktə]	管理者			
10	expert [ékspəːrt]	専門家			
11	fisherman [fíʃəmən]	漁師			
12	grocer [gróusər]	食料雑貨商			
13	housewife [háuswaif]	主婦			
14	president [prézidənt]	大統領			
15	professor [prəfésər]	教授			
16	soldier [sóuldʒər]	兵士			

● 人間関係　ジャンル別 16 (p. 245)

No.	単語	意味	書きこみ①	書きこみ②	書きこみ③
1	boss [bɔ́(ː)s]	上司			
2	coworker [kóuwərkər]	同僚			
3	dad [dǽd]	とうさん			
4	grandchild [grǽntʃaild]	孫			
5	grand-parents [grǽnpeərənts]	祖父母			
6	kinship [kínʃip]	親類関係			
7	Majesty [mǽdʒəsti]	陛下			
8	marital [mǽərətl]	夫婦の			
9	mom [mάm]	かあさん			
10	sir [sɔ́ːr]	お客様			
11	spouse [spáus]	配偶者			

No.	単語	意味	書きこみ①	書きこみ②	書きこみ③
1	**bank** [bǽŋk]	土手			
2	**canyon** [kǽnjən]	深い渓谷			
3	**cape** [kéip]	岬			
4	**cave** [kéiv]	洞窟			
5	**channel** [tʃǽnl]	海峡			
6	**cliff** [klíf]	がけ			
7	**coast** [kóust]	沿岸地帯			
8	**coral reef** [kɔ́:rəl ri:f]	珊瑚礁			
9	**countryside** [kʌ́ntrisaid]	田園			
10	**fountain** [fáuntn]	泉			
11	**glacier** [gléiʃər]	氷河			
12	**gulf** [gʌ́lf]	湾			
13	**harbor** [há:rbər]	港			
14	**iceberg** [áisbə:rg]	氷山			
15	**lava** [lá:və]	溶岩			
16	**oasis** [ouéisis]	オアシス			
17	**peninsula** [pənínsələ]	半島			
18	**plain** [pléin]	平野			
19	**pond** [pánd]	池			
20	**port** [pɔ́:rt]	港			
21	**reservoir** [rézərvwa:r]	貯水池			
22	**sanctuary** [sǽŋktʃueri]	禁漁区			
23	**swamp** [swámp]	沼地			
24	**valley** [vǽli]	谷			
25	**waterfall** [wɔ́:tərfɔ:l]	滝			

● 地名　ジャンル別 18 (p. 268)

No.	単語	意味	書きこみ①	書きこみ②	書きこみ③
1	the Antarctic [æntά:rktik]	南極地方			
2	the Arctic [ά:rktik]	北極地方			
3	the Atlantic Ocean [ətlǽntik]	大西洋			
4	the Mediter-ranean Sea [meditəréiniən]	地中海			
5	the North Pole [nɔ́:rθ póul]	北極			
6	the Pacific Ocean [pəsífik]	太平洋			
7	the South Pole [sάuθ póul]	南極			

● 物質　ジャンル別 19 (p. 280)

No.	単語	意味	書きこみ①	書きこみ②	書きこみ③
1	aluminum [əlú:mənəm]	アルミニウム			
2	bronze [bránz]	青銅			
3	carbohydrate [kɑ:rbouháidreit]	炭水化物			
4	chlorine [klɔ́:ri:n]	塩素			
5	coal [kóul]	炭			
6	copper [kάpər]	銅			
7	crystal [krístl]	水晶			
8	iron [áiərn]	鉄			
9	ivory [áivəri]	ぞうげ			
10	lead [léd]	鉛			
11	marble [mάəbl]	大理石			
12	methane [méθein]	メタン			
13	ore [ɔ́:]	鉱石			
14	pearl [pə́:l]	真珠			
15	silver [sílvər]	銀			
16	sodium [sóudiəm]	ナトリウム			
17	steel [stí:l]	鋼鉄			
18	sulfur [sʌ́lfər]	硫黄			

★ ジャンル別

● 天体　ジャンル別 20 (p. 291)

No.	単語	意味	書きこみ①	書きこみ②	書きこみ③
1	**asteroid** [ǽstərɔid]	小惑星			
2	**comet** [kάmit]	すい星			
3	**meteor** [mí:tiə]	流星			
4	**planet** [plǽnit]	惑星			
5	**satellite** [sǽtəlait]	衛星			
6	**the Milky Way**	銀河			

● 植物②　ジャンル別 21 (p. 322)

No.	単語	意味	書きこみ①	書きこみ②	書きこみ③
1	**bud** [bʌ́d]	つぼみ			
2	**bulb** [bʌ́lb]	球根			
3	**dandelion** [dǽndəlaiən]	タンポポ			
4	**graft** [grǽft]	接ぎ木			
5	**hydrangea** [haidréindʒə]	アジサイ			
6	**iris** [áiəris]	アイリス			
7	**orchid** [ɔ́:rkəd]	ラン			
8	**petal** [pétl]	花びら			
9	**pollen** [pάlən]	花粉			
10	**sprout** [spráut]	芽			
11	**thorn** [θɔ́:rn]	トゲ			
12	**trunk** [trʌ́ŋk]	幹			
13	**turf** [tə́:rf]	芝地			
14	**twig** [twíg]	小枝			

● 病気・けが　ジャンル別 22 (p. 322)

No.	単語	意味	書きこみ①	書きこみ②	書きこみ③
1	**allergy** [ǽlədʒi]	アレルギー			
2	**asthma** [ǽzmə]	ぜんそく			
3	**bruise** [brúːz]	打撲傷			
4	**cholera** [kálərə]	コレラ			
5	**diabetes** [daiəbíːtiːz]	糖尿病			
6	**diarrhea** [daiəríːə]	下痢			
7	**epilepsy** [épəlepsi]	てんかん			
8	**flu** [flúː]	インフルエンザ			
9	**fracture** [frǽktʃə]	骨折			
10	**leukemia** [lu(ː)kíːmiə]	白血病			
11	**malaria** [məléəriə]	マラリア			
12	**neurosis** [njuəróusis]	ノイローゼ			
13	**pneumonia** [njumóunjə]	肺炎			
14	**scar** [skáːr]	傷跡			
15	**smallpox** [smɔ́ːlpɑks]	天然痘			
16	**tuberculosis** [tjubəːkjəlóusis]	結核			

● 教育　ジャンル別 23 (p. 357)

No.	単語	意味	書きこみ①	書きこみ②	書きこみ③
1	**admission** [ədmíʃən]	入学			
2	**applicant** [ǽplikənt]	志願者			
3	**bachelor** [bǽtʃələr]	学士			
4	**credit** [krédit]	単位			
5	**curriculum** [kəríkjələm]	カリキュラム			
6	**degree** [digríː]	学位			
7	**department** [dipáːrtmənt]	学部			
8	**diploma** [diplóumə]	卒業証書			
9	**dorm** [dɔ́ːrm]	寮			

ジャンル別

10	**enrollment** [enróulmən]	入学			
11	**freshman** [fréʃmən]	新入生			
12	**graduate** [grǽdʒuət]	大学卒業生			
13	**handout** [hǽndaut]	プリント			
14	**lecture** [léktʃər]	講義			
15	**major** [méidʒər]	専攻			
16	**material** [mətíəriəl]	資料			
17	**office hours**	研究室在室時間			
18	**photocopy** [fóutoukɑpi]	コピー			
19	**qualified** [kwɑ́ləfàid]	資格のある			
20	**quiz** [kwíz]	小テスト			
21	**recommendation** [rèkəməndéiʃən]	推薦(状)			
22	**requirement** [rikwáiərmənt]	必要条件			
23	**scholarship** [skɑ́lərʃip]	奨学金			
24	**semester** [səméstər]	学期			
25	**sophomore** [sɑ́fəmɔ̀ːr]	2年生			
26	**syllabus** [síləbəs]	シラバス			
27	**term** [tə́ːrm]	学期			
28	**tuition** [tju(ː)íʃən]	授業(料)			
29	**tutor** [tjúːtər]	個別指導教員			
30	**undergraduate** [ʌndərgrǽdʒuət]	大学生			

No.	単語	意味	書きこみ①	書きこみ②	書きこみ③
☐					
☐					
☐					
☐					
☐					
☐					
☐					
☐					
☐					
☐					
☐					
☐					
☐					
☐					
☐					
☐					
☐					
☐					
☐					
☐					
☐					
☐					
☐					
☐					
☐					

★オリジナルの単語リストを作って3回書きこみしよう!★

No.	単語	意味	書きこみ①	書きこみ②	書きこみ③
☐					
☐					
☐					
☐					
☐					
☐					
☐					
☐					
☐					
☐					
☐					
☐					
☐					
☐					
☐					
☐					
☐					
☐					
☐					
☐					
☐					
☐					
☐					
☐					
☐					
☐					

★オリジナルの単語リストを作って3回書きこみしよう！★

No.	単語	意味	書きこみ①	書きこみ②	書きこみ③
☐					
☐					
☐					
☐					
☐					
☐					
☐					
☐					
☐					
☐					
☐					
☐					
☐					
☐					
☐					
☐					
☐					
☐					
☐					
☐					
☐					
☐					
☐					
☐					
☐					

★オリジナルの単語リストを作って3回書きこみしよう！★

No.	単語	意味	書きこみ①	書きこみ②	書きこみ③
☐					
☐					
☐					
☐					
☐					
☐					
☐					
☐					
☐					
☐					
☐					
☐					
☐					
☐					
☐					
☐					
☐					
☐					
☐					
☐					
☐					
☐					
☐					
☐					
☐					
☐					

1回目 　／　　2回目 　／　　3回目 　／

★オリジナルの単語リストを作って3回書きこみしよう！★

システム英単語〈5訂版対応〉

フレーズ・単語書きこみワークブック

著　　　者	霜　　康司
	刀祢　雅彦
発　行　者	山﨑　良子
印刷・製本	株式会社日本制作センター

発　行　所　　駿台文庫株式会社

〒101-0062　東京都千代田区神田駿河台1-7-4

小畑ビル内

TEL. 編集 03(5259)3302

販売 03(5259)3301

《③－192pp.》

ISBN978-4-7961-1140-9　　Printed in Japan